UNIQUELY YOU

For Quiet Trailblazers & Creative Navigators

BY RUTH BRUNNER

UNIQUELY YOU

"A warm, empowering guide to turning obstacles into openings and honouring the quiet strength of your unique journey."

— ***Shannon Anima, Trauma-Informed Psychotherapist/Writer***

First published by Ultimate World Publishing 2025
Copyright © 2025 Ruth Brunner

ISBN

Paperback: 978-1-923425-69-9
Ebook: 978-1-923425-70-5

Ruth Brunner has asserted her rights under the Copyright, Designs and Patents Act 1988 to be identified as the author of this work. The information in this book is based on the author's experiences and opinions. The publisher specifically disclaims responsibility for any adverse consequences which may result from use of the information contained herein. Permission to use information has been sought by the author. Any breaches will be rectified in further editions of the book.

All rights reserved. No part of this publication may be reproduced, stored in or introduced into a retrieval system, or transmitted in any form, or by any means (electronic, mechanical, photocopying, recording or otherwise) without the prior written permission of the author. Any person who does any unauthorised act in relation to this publication may be liable to criminal prosecution and civil claims for damages. Enquiries should be made through the publisher.

Cover design: Ultimate World Publishing
Layout and typesetting: Ultimate World Publishing
Editor: Victoria Pickens

Ultimate World Publishing
Diamond Creek,
Victoria Australia 3089
www.writeabook.com.au

Keynotes for Readers

About "Creative Snapshots"

Throughout the book, you'll find Creative Snapshots — short, illustrative stories aligned with the theme of each chapter. These scenarios are inspired by real-life possibilities and tailored from the author's observations, experiences, and understanding of the human journey.

Designed to evoke authentic emotions and reflections, these stories blend imagination with universal truths to spark connection and offer meaningful examples. While not literal accounts of actual events or individuals, they are intended to illuminate the ideas shared in this book and to encourage self-exploration.

Any resemblance to actual persons, living or dead, or to real events, is purely coincidental.

Flow-Inspired Creations & Flowcrafting

Throughout this book, the terms Flow-Inspired Creations and flowcrafting are used interchangeably in a purely descriptive context. They refer to personal, creative approaches designed to foster intuitive self-expression and creativity in a state of flow. Neither term is intended to represent or imply trademark status or affiliation with any other entities, brands, or practices. Any resemblance to other existing terms or commercial uses is purely coincidental.

Anchored in a Sign

This symbol featured in this book represents the journey of Align, Create, Reframe & Thrive. Like a star radiating from a centred core, it embodies the energy that arises from finding inner connection, expressing creativity, shifting perspectives, and flourishing outwardly. This emblem appears at the close of each chapter as a reminder of our shared becoming.

A Note on Flow-Inspired Reflections

Scattered throughout this book are verses — poetic pauses I've written to mark a moment or offer a question. I call them *Flow-Inspired Reflections*. They arose through writing, noticing, and listening. May they quietly stir your own voice into motion.

Endnotes – explaining meaning

You'll notice small superscript numbers next to a few words throughout the book. These markers lead to clarifications and reflections gathered at the end of the book in the *Endnotes*.

Disclaimer

This book is intended for educational and inspirational purposes only. It is not a substitute for professional medical, psychological, or therapeutic advice, diagnosis, or treatment.

The practices and reflections shared are based on personal experience and are not clinically tested for the treatment, prevention, or management of specific conditions. If you have concerns about your physical, emotional, or mental well-being, please seek support from a qualified healthcare professional.

By engaging with the Flow-Inspired Creation exercises, readers acknowledge that they do so at their own discretion and accept full responsibility for their personal experiences and outcomes.

You are encouraged to approach all practices with self-awareness, gentleness, and care.

Testimonials

Here's what Early Readers Are Saying:

"A warm and practical guide for anyone interested in personal development with wise counsel on turning obstacles into openings and challenges into resilience. An insightful approach to honouring your unique life path and claiming freedom from judgments and powerlessness."
— *Shannon Anima,*
Trauma-informed Psychotherapist/Writer

"I especially loved the Prelude written in verse and flow. Ruth captures feelings so evocatively and honestly, creating a deeply touching and memorable opening.

Her book is a gift, offering us a variety of artistic forms to use as tools for healing and grounding. It's something to turn to whenever life feels chaotic and overwhelming."
— *Nadia R.*

"Uniquely You is a transformative guide that helps readers connect with their inner strengths through practical, creative exercises. Through personal stories of overcoming

disenfranchisement, Ruth illustrates how reframing one's narrative can foster belonging and purpose. With its emphasis on diversity as a source of richness, the book offers varied approaches to suit different personalities, encouraging collaboration and community-building.
Its approachable tone and relatable storytelling make it meaningful and accessible for anyone, regardless of artistic experience."

— Rashmi P.

Your thoughts matter! If this book has inspired or resonated with you, I'd love to hear your feedback — on my website or via this form at:

https://www.flow-inspired-creations.com.au/feedback-future-interest/

Dedication

To all those who have ever felt out of place and dared to be different — this book is for you.

Every person is a masterpiece, both in being and becoming.

You are not defined by the labels or expectations placed upon you.

You are the storyteller of your life, and your creativity holds the power to transform, connect, and thrive.

May this book awaken the quiet strength found within, the gentle power of adapting to life's winds, and the beauty of celebrating your uniqueness – your greatest gift. May it also inspire you to rediscover a sense of belonging by daring to belong through being different, and thriving by standing tall in your unapologetic self.

Uniquely You

A Welcome Gift for You

A Room of Your Own Making
A gentle beginning, just for you.

You've just picked up *Uniquely You*, and I'm truly glad you're here.

Before we go any further, I'd love to offer you a small gift:

A quiet place to begin, especially if you've ever felt like you didn't quite fit.

A Room of Your Own Making is a free companion guide — an invitation to reconnect with your uniqueness and begin shaping a space where you belong not because you've adapted, but because you've arrived as you are.

Thank you for arriving here — exactly as you are. Let this be your first step into the room that's always been waiting — the one you're free to make your own.

Inside, you'll find:
A reflection to anchor yourself in what's true
A creative prompt to begin shaping your own space of becoming
A gentle mindset shift: You don't need to fit in to belong

A Welcome Gift for You

This is your moment to begin — not perfectly, but presently. Download your free bonus gift here: https://www.flow-inspired-creations.com.au/a-room-of-your-own-making/

Contents

Beginnings

- **Testimonials** — ix
  Early readers share their impressions.

- **Keynotes for Readers** — v
  Context and invitation, before you begin.

- **Dedication** — xi
  A personal acknowledgment.

- **A Welcome Gift for You** *(Special Bonus)* — xii
  An invitation to nurture your own creative space.

- **Foreword by Dr Rob Garbutt** — 1
  An opening reflection from a trusted voice.

Prelude: Stories in Verse and Flow — 5
A poetic invitation—where stories meet the rhythm of flow.

- Whispers of Becoming — 5
- Facing the Past — 8
- Finding Agency — 9
- Lifeline of Creativity — 11

Chapters

Chapter 1. Unspooling the Thread: Starting Exactly Where You Are   23
Beginning your journey exactly where life finds you.

- The Possibility of You   23
- Stepping into Flow   26
- Quiet Trailblazers and Creative Navigators   35
- Belonging: The Courage to Be Exactly Who You Are   37

Chapter 2. Setting the Stage: Turning Scars Into Stories   45
Finding treasures in past experiences.

- Threads of Origin   45
- Flow, Before I Had a Name for It   51
- Reframing Kinship   56
- From Scars to Strength: Threads of Transformation   60

Chapter 3. The Place I Went to Make Sense   63
Discovering self through creative play.

- The Birth of "Flow-Inspired Mind Play"   63
- Golden Seams, Bold Stories   68
- Inner Reflections, Outer Patterns   69
- Opening the Practice Window   71

Chapter 4. When Silence Makes a Sound   83
Exploring the hidden resonance of silence.

- Sound Beneath the Silence   83
- Embracing My Sound: A Personal Path to Flow   84
- The Melodies That Move Us   86
- Soundscapes of Self: Crafting New Stories   86

Contents

Chapter 5. When Symbols Speak — 97
Symbols as gateways to deeper understanding.

- The Nature of Belief — 97
- Raindrops of Change: A New Vision for Myself — 98
- Symbols: A Gateway to Self-Discovery — 100
- When Symbols Meet Flow — 103

Chapter 6. Becoming in the Not-Yet-Known — 115
Leaning into uncertainty and creative freedom.

- Leaning into Creative Freedom: Dreamscapes — 115
- Allowing and Becoming: Embracing Freedom Through Flow — 117
- Room for Beauty in Uncertainty — 118
- Finding Joy in Unpredictability — 119

Chapter 7. Weaving Life's Threads — 133
Crafting identity and resilience through fibres of meaning.

- Fibres of Identity: Crafting Stories in the Weave — 133
- Resilient Threads: Weaving My Life Narrative — 135
- Threads of Becoming — 138
- Reflections in the Weave: Threads of Storytelling — 140

Chapter 8. Drawing Calm From Chaos — 151
Using structured creativity for clarity.

- Structured Patterns: A Creative Sanctuary — 151
- Tracing the Lines: How Patterns Carve Clarity — 152
- Flow Lines: Patterns as Guides to Insight — 153
- Snapshot: Flowing Into Self-Acceptance — 160

Chapter 9. Writing Without Edges — **167**
Expressing freely, beyond constraints.

- Unleashing the Flow: Writing Without Boundaries — 168
- The Art of Letting Go: My Experience of Flowcrafting with Words — 169
- Opening the Creative Floodgates — 173
- Snapshot: Writing Toward Clarity — 176

Chapter 10. Fleeting Wonders: Nature as Muse — **183**
Discovering belonging through nature's wisdom.

- Nature: The Ultimate Artist — 183
- Nature as Path to Belonging — 187
- My Early Influence: 'Grossvati' and the Magic of Nature — 189
- Snapshot: Flowcrafting in Collaboration with Nature — 206

Chapter 11: Cultural Currents: Flowing Through Us — **211**
How cultures shape our creative journey.

- Culture as a Creative Lens — 211
- Immersed in Culture: How India Steered My Course — 213
- Sacred Notes: A Cultural Tapestry of Chanting — 218
- Snapshot: A Heritage Remembered, A Story Rewoven — 225

Epilogue: Flowcrafting Tomorrow's Stories — **231**
Looking forward with creative resilience.

- Unwritten Skies — An Offering for Your Path Ahead — 236

Contents

About the Author   **237**
Meet the author behind these reflections.

Acknowledgements   **239**
Expressing gratitude to those who shaped this journey.

From Story to Offering   **241**
Continuing your exploration beyond this book.

Speaker Bio   **242**

What Waits Beyond These Pages   **243**
Invitations and pathways for further engagement.

End Notes   **249**
References and additional insights.

Foreword

Ruth Brunner's *Uniquely You* is inspirational and practical. It combines personal storytelling, by an experienced counsellor, with creative exercises: exercises that begin with where you are and that encourage interconnections to develop with others, human and more-than-human.

I was drawn into Ruth's creative process when supervising the Bachelor of Arts (Honours) research from which this book emerged. In Australia, an Honours degree requires completion of an intense, full-time, year-long research project which is supervised by an experienced researcher. As Ruth's supervisor, I met with her regularly to discuss how the research was going.

Ruth's research, titled *Ephemera*, was personal, deeply exploratory and creative. Explorations always start uncertainly, which was fitting for *Ephemera*, a plural noun meaning 'one who, or something which, has a transitory existence'. And I have to say that, at first, I was uncertain about Ruth's focus on 'ephemera'. But this wasn't my problem to figure out, and as we say, 'trust in the process'.

Ruth began her exploration guided by a research process called autoethnography. Think of 'auto' as 'self', like an automobile appears to be mobile all by its self. 'Ethnography', on the other hand, is what anthropologists do when they write about the people and cultures they observe. So autoethnography is writing about yourself as if you were an anthropologist observing your life.

This might seem to be a self-indulgent activity, however, when we engage with this way of researching, we write through the lens of social justice not only of ourselves but also of our time, our culture, our place in it and our experience of it. Autoethnography is a method that makes meaning of one's life as a unique being interconnected with one's world.

Ruth began by writing about the ephemeral creative works she made each day: how they came about, and the meanings they held for her at that place and time. In her typical way, this work proceeded like a bright, swiftly-flowing, clear stream. But something murky stirred, around a bend, in a rock pool.

This stirring came in the form of a genogram, Ruth's kinship diagram. It represented an aspect of Ruth's life experience that she had decided to exclude from her research, but it insisted on its relevance. In her words, and as she explains in this book, the kinship diagram put on show 'the absence of kinship in my life'. A detached leaf in free fall. No tree.

Ephemera, as the keyword in Ruth's research, began to make sense for me, because facing this image is a stark and unsettling reminder that our existence is ephemeral. It also raises questions of how we belong in this world. Family, after all, is so often emphasised as a primary and lasting location of belonging that extends from us here-and-now to our past kin and to the kinfolk of our future.

By chance, I had been reading a book called *Staying with the Trouble* by Donna Haraway when we met after Ruth had first faced this kinship diagram. In it, Donna Haraway writes about 'making kin' and she extends possible kinship connections beyond our species to all earthlings. I suggested having a read.

Haraway's ideas took life in Ruth's project which, in a metaphoric sense, was about making kinship connections with materials to create artistic offspring. Her reflective writing began to reframe belonging as a creative practice of making kin. Here — thinking with ideas developed by Elspeth Probyn in *Outside Belonging* — belonging is no longer understood as our passive inclusion in a group. Instead, it is something that emerges through active and ongoing processes of being made. Belonging is something or, more accurately, many things that we do.

As she continued her creative practice and reflection, with Haraway in her backpack, Ruth began reframing the problem the genogram had presented. Instead of missing connections, new ones came into being.

This gives just a small glimpse of the transformative processes and insights Ruth shares in this book. Beginning with personal story, Ruth has drawn on her experience to create practical exercises to take you on your own path of self-discovery, creative growth, and reframing personal narratives.

In *Uniquely You* Ruth's deep reflection on the incredibly difficult challenges in her life, are turned generously outwards. It offers engaging storytelling with actionable exercises that will empower you to find meaning, connection, and self-expression.

Creativity has been profoundly therapeutic in Ruth's journey, and *Uniquely You* provides a path to making creativity an indispensable part of yours.

It has been a joy to see where Ruth's research has led her, and how it continues to thrive.

Rob Garbutt, PhD,
January 2025.

Prelude: Stories in Verse and Flow

Before the journey begins, let me share fragments of my story — moments of clarity, resilience, and connection. These verses and creative narratives are a glimpse of Flow-Inspired Creation in motion — a tapestry of reflections woven from my life, offering a moment to pause, reflect, and embark on a creative walk. Let them guide you into the flow of what lies ahead.

Whispers of Becoming

She stands at the edges,
a quiet trailblazer, a seeker of truth
where shadows linger and light dances.
Life taught her to carry scars like whispers,
etched into her soul yet softened
by the art of resilience.

Once, the weight of silence fell heavy.
Alone, on a rolled-up rug, she wept,
unable to see the tapestry of good
woven into the threads of her life.

Uniquely You

What seemed unbreakable within her fractured,
but even in that fracture, there was a seed —
a seed of belonging, waiting for a place to grow.

Through unexpected doorways, she found her way:
a newspaper ad promising philosophy,
a group of strangers who became a harbour,
and a teacher — a former monk —
who taught her the language of stillness.
"Go through it," he said, "not over it."
And so, she journeyed inward,
finding not a cure but a rhythm,
a way to dance with the darkness
and make peace with its steps.

Time shaped her understanding.
The words of wise men and healers became her anchors.
She learnt of a malleable brain,
rewired through attention and intention,
where old stories of inadequacy
gave way to songs of strength.
What once seemed ephemeral — fleeting moments,
brief connections — became her compass.

The fragility of life became her teacher,
death its shadowed companion.
She turned toward this impermanence,
not as a void,
but as a reminder to live fully,
to grasp the threads of passing moments
and weave them into meaning.

Prelude: Stories in Verse and Flow

She rewrote the script handed to her:
from "not enough" to "capable,"
from "disconnected" to "belonging."
Through gratitude, she found flourishing;
through mindfulness, she found stillness;
through storytelling, she found freedom.

Her search for meaning was never linear —
it twisted and turned, paused and began anew.
Through the absurdity of Kafka[1],
the wisdom of Yalom[2],
and the steady guidance of source,
she uncovered the vastness of her inner world.
Belonging, she learnt,
was not confined to a place or a person,
but could grow from the soil of connection —
to self, to others, to something greater.

And now, she invites you into this story:
to walk with her through the ephemera,
to see how cracks become mosaics,
how the fleeting becomes eternal,
and how the courage to belong
can transform the quietest of whispers
into a resounding song.

---

[1] Franz Kafka (1883–1924) was a Czech-born writer whose works, like *The Metamorphosis* and *The Trial*, explore themes of alienation and existential angst, influencing modern literature.

[2] Irvin D. Yalom (b. 1931) is an existential psychiatrist and author known for integrating existential philosophy into psychotherapy. His works, such as *Existential Psychotherapy* and *The Gift of Therapy*, explore themes of meaning, mortality, and human connection.

A Bird's-Eye View: Tracing the Threads

What shapes a life?
Is it the stories we are told, or the stories we tell ourselves?
For me, life has been a tapestry of broken threads and quiet reinvention,
each frayed edge teaching me
that meaning is not found — it is made.

Facing the Past

The oaks stood tall, unmoving, as I returned to the place I had long avoided.

Wartheim[3]. The avenue, beautiful as a postcard, portrayed
no trace of the girl I had been.
Fear and hesitation clung to me as I stood before its door.
But as I knocked and spoke,
I found not the ghosts I had feared,
but a quiet revelation:

The past, though it shapes us, does not define us.
The weight I carried began to dissolve,
its ephemerality revealed.

---

[3] *Wartheim*, located in Muri bei Bern, was one of the first homes for "difficult to manage" children in Switzerland, founded in 1862. Over the years, its purpose evolved, originally serving as a facility for the destitute, the ill, and those in need of correction or disciplinary care, before transitioning to a home focused on structured upbringing. It still operates today, though under new management.

This was my first epiphany:
What has been can become what no longer is.

Finding Agency

In time, I learnt that freedom lies in choice:
the choice to reframe, to rewrite, to reach for better-feeling thoughts.
From the wisdom of therapists, philosophers, and sages,
I gathered tools to dismantle the stories that no longer served me.
I discovered the power of small steps:
A thought that feels just a little lighter.
A memory held with just a little less pain.

Gratitude and mindfulness became my companions,
showing me that even the darkest moments
can hold the seeds of transformation.

This was my second epiphany:
We are not the victims of our stories — we are their authors.

Wisdom from the World

India whispered truths into my soul:
What is, is temporary. What will be, is unwritten.
The Yogis taught me to live in the fleeting *now*,
to hold joy and sorrow lightly,
to embrace the possibility of change.

This wisdom became my compass.
By shifting my attention,
I rewired the patterns of my mind,
finding strength where I once saw weakness.

This was my third epiphany:
Our thoughts shape our worlds, and the worlds we shape can free us.

Prelude: Stories in Verse and Flow

Lifeline of Creativity

When words failed me, art spoke.
Through ink and colour, shape and texture,
I found a way to express what my voice could not.
Visual narratives became my lifelines —
guiding me through the untold stories
I did not yet know how to tell.

Art taught me to listen to the whispers of my own becoming,
to see beauty in what is unfinished,
to trust the process of creating.

This was my fourth epiphany:
Creativity is not a product; it is a way of being.

An Invitation

These moments, these learnings, are but glimpses.
I share them not to dwell on the past,
but to offer a bridge to the present —
to the *you* reading these words.

What stories do you carry?
What threads will you weave into your own tapestry?
Together, let us explore how scars can become mosaics,
how the ephemeral can be eternal,
and how belonging can be found
within ourselves, and through creation.

Echoes from Facing the Past

The train hummed quietly beneath me as the countryside rolled by, its greens and browns blurring into a memory I wasn't sure I was ready to face. Wartheim[4]. I hadn't said the name aloud in years, but now it sat heavy on my tongue, unspoken but present, like a ghost in the corner of the room.

The avenue of oaks stretched out before me, as stately as I remembered. It was strange, how beautiful it looked now, its symmetry so perfect, its silence so complete. Yet my heart pounded. My feet hesitated. The girl I had been — raking leaves, carrying shame — stood in my mind's eye, as vivid as if she were still there.

But as I walked down that familiar path, something shifted. The oaks whispered a truth I had long ignored:

The past, though it shapes us, does not define us. What has been can become what no longer is.

At the door, my hand trembled. "Just tell them you were here as a child," Dr S had said, but my voice felt trapped. Finally, the door opened, and a friendly woman smiled, unaware of the storm raging inside me. As we spoke, I felt it: the weight of *Wartheim* lifting. It was no longer mine to carry.

I walked away lighter, and for the first time in years, I truly believed:

---

[4] *See Footnote 3*

Scars are not the end of the story. They are the beginning of transformation.

Echoes from Finding Agency

The rickshaw rattled through the narrow streets of *Brahmpuri*[5], its small engine struggling to keep pace with the life teeming around us. The blue walls stretched upward, sun-faded and cracked, their colour as vivid as the stories I imagined they held. My eyes wandered, taking in the quiet hum of this corner of Jodhpur — still untouched by Western tourists, still brimming with an untamed energy.

I had come here seeking something. Perhaps peace. Perhaps belonging. But instead, the streets had given me stones, thrown from rooftops, and whispers of *"Angrich*[6]*"* that cut sharper than I expected. And now this.

---

[5] *Brahmpuri* is a historic Brahmin-dominated neighbourhood in Jodhpur, Rajasthan, known for its traditional blue-painted houses. Situated near the Mehrangarh Fort, it reflects the cultural and architectural heritage of the city, with its narrow lanes and vibrant community life.

[6] *Angrich*: A colloquial term used in India, derived from "English," historically referring to British colonizers and, by extension, often used for any white Western foreigners. Given Britain's centuries-long rule over India, the term carried a lingering stigma, associating white foreigners with the legacy of colonial rule and oppression.

Prelude: Stories in Verse and Flow

The moment came so fast I barely registered it. A passer-by turned, his face unreadable, and spat.

The spit hit my face before I could look away, and the world stopped.

I froze, my breath catching in my chest as the rickshaw bumped along. I couldn't speak. Couldn't think. I only felt the humiliation — the sharp sting of rejection, as if I didn't deserve to share the space I inhabited.

When I finally reached my room, the tears came. I sat on the hard floor, head in my hands, and sobbed. The shame was overwhelming. It felt like being a child again, told I didn't matter, told I wasn't wanted. The walls around me, so blue and full of life, now felt like they were closing in.

And then, in the quiet of my despair, a voice stirred. It wasn't loud, nor did it drown out my pain. It whispered, steady and calm, somewhere between my head and my heart:
You have a choice.

At first, I ignored it. The sting of the moment was too fresh. But the voice returned, insistent now:
A choice to reach for a thought that feels just a little lighter.

The idea seemed absurd. My cheeks were still damp, my skin still burned with shame. Yet slowly, I felt myself reaching — tentatively, haltingly — for something gentler. A memory, distant but clear, surfaced: a time of kindness, of connection, of feeling seen.

It didn't erase what had happened. But it softened it. And as I held onto that thread of light, I realised something:

Even in the darkest moments,
there are seeds of transformation waiting to take root.
We are not the victims of our stories — we are their authors.

The walls of *Brahmpuri*, with their faded paint and perfect imperfection, no longer felt like barriers. They became a mirror — reflecting not just my pain, but my resilience. The streets hummed as they always had, their energy unchanging. But something in me had shifted.

I stood, brushed myself off, and stepped outside.
This wasn't about forgetting or pretending the pain wasn't real.
It was about choosing how I carried it,
about deciding what story I would write next.

Prelude: Stories in Verse and Flow

Echoes from Lifeline of Creativity

The bistro was alive with life, a cacophony of clinking glasses, bursts of laughter, and the scrape of chairs on tiled floors. Around me, groups of diners leaned into each other, their conversations swirling in languages I didn't understand. I sat alone at a small table, waiting. For who, I can't even remember now.

Whoever it was didn't show up.

Awareness of my solitude grew louder with each passing minute. I shifted awkwardly, my hands resting on the table as I tried to appear at ease. But the truth sat heavy in my chest: I felt exposed, like I didn't belong in this bustling world of connection and togetherness.

I ordered a drink to occupy my hands, then reached into my bag. My fingers found the small square of 10x10cm paper and the familiar slim shape of my Sakura Micron pen.

I started to draw.

At first, it was simply something to do —
a way to avoid staring at the door,
to quiet the part of me
that felt awkward and out of place.

Lines became patterns,
patterns became rhythms,
and soon the noise of the bistro faded.
The world beyond my paper fell away.

I didn't notice the little girl until her voice broke through. "What are you doing?"

I looked up, startled. She stood beside my table, her dark eyes wide with curiosity. Behind her, a family filled a larger table, their conversation spilling out in joyous bursts.

"I'm drawing," I said, turning my square toward her.

Her face lit up. "Can you show me?"

For a moment, I hesitated. Would her parents mind? But the eagerness in her eyes nudged me forward. I smiled and tilted the paper toward her, explaining the patterns I had started.

"Can I do it?" she asked, her voice bright with hope.

"Of course," I said, pulling out another blank square from my bag. I sketched a few guiding lines with my pencil, handed it to her, and pointed toward her table.

"Go ask your parents for a pen," I said gently. "And draw your own patterns. You'll see — it's fun."

She skipped away, clutching the paper like a treasure. I quickly scribbled a website on the back, something her parents could use to find more ideas if she wanted to keep going.

I returned to my own square, the pen gliding effortlessly over the paper, and let my thoughts quiet once more.

Prelude: Stories in Verse and Flow

Listen to the whispers of your own becoming.

―――

Out of the corner of my eye, I saw her at her table,
hunched over her square,
her family watching as she worked,
her small face alive with joy.

In her delight, I saw it:
beauty in what was unfinished,
a reminder that nothing is ever truly complete.

The lines I drew weren't just marks on paper.
They were a bridge —
a connection,
a moment shared between strangers.

And in that moment, I felt it again, as if the patterns themselves were speaking:

Creativity is not a product; it is a way of being.

―――

The bistro remained as noisy and alive as before,
but my table no longer felt empty.
I wasn't waiting anymore.

Instead, I was exactly where I needed to be.

From fragments of becoming to pathways of possibility — let's begin the experience of Flow-Inspired Creations together.

Prelude: Stories in Verse and Flow

Image 1 **"Lifeline of Creativity"** –
Collage composed by the author, blending
digital elements with creative vision.

Unspooling the Thread: Starting Exactly Where You Are

*"Follow the thread that feels quietly true —
not to unravel, but to bring what's waiting into view."*

— *Flow-Inspired Reflection*

This opening thread offers a glimpse of what lies ahead — a chance to orient, to settle, and to feel into the rhythm of what this book can offer.

The Possibility of You

Uniquely You is an invitation to explore, discover, and play. To align with your inner flow and allow it to guide you toward what is uniquely yours. Throughout these pages, I share my own stories, explorations, and the creative practices that have influenced me — not because they are the answers, but because they offer possibilities. Flow-Inspired Creations, whether through words, sound, fibres, or culture, have never been just about the medium itself. They have been about connection, aligning with something deeper, something already within me, waiting to be expressed.

Perhaps you, too, have felt different, as if the very things that set you apart have made belonging difficult. But what if those differences are not barriers, but gifts? What if creativity is not merely an activity, but a way of being — one that brings you closer to what truly engages and fulfils you? My hope is that, within these stories and explorations, you discover a spark — an opening into your own calling, your own rhythm of expressing who you are. There is no single right way, only what feels alive to you. This is your invitation to step into flow, to trust in your unique rhythm, and to create from the essence of who you are.

Flow-Inspired Creations are at the heart of this book — not as a set of instructions, but as an invitation to engage with creativity as a living experience. This is a space for exploration, where curiosity, creativity and personal discovery converge.

There's no predefined mould to fit into. Flow is about allowing yourself to move freely, trusting what resonates, and stepping into the possibilities that lie ahead.

This journey is yours. Flow is yours. Let's begin.

How This Book Found Its Way to You

Imagine a pathway, not one made of bricks and mortar, but one forged by imagination, courage, and the quiet strength that already resides within you. This is a path back to yourself — an unfolding alignment with your natural rhythm, where the very things that once set you apart hold hidden possibilities. Strengths can then reveal themselves, and your uniqueness begins to shine.

This book is your guide along that path. Through reflections, Flow-Inspired Creations — at times referred to as flowcrafting — and creative explorations, each chapter invites you to step into a process of discovery. These practices aren't about fixing what's broken; they're about uncovering what's already whole — possibilities waiting to be expressed through creativity.

Like an artisan crafting their creations, you'll learn to approach your story with intention, imagination, and self-compassion. I use the words "story" and "narrative" throughout the book because, often, the way we see ourselves — our differences, our ways of thinking, our unique approaches to life — have been formed by the stories we've been told or the ones we've told ourselves.

Reframing our narratives isn't just about changing words; it's about recognising that these stories are, at their core, beliefs. And beliefs can shift, expand, and open new possibilities. Whether it's the way your mind works, the way you create, or the way you move through the world, I want to show you — through my own experiences and the creative exercises in this book — that difference is not something to be fixed or hidden. It is something to be honoured.

This isn't merely a creative process — it's a journey of becoming. Together, let's explore how the flow within you can lead to clarity, connection, and the courage to fully embrace who you truly are.

This book found its way to you because you are ready to shine in your uniqueness — to step fully into your creativity, embrace your inner flow, and express the fullness of who you are.

Stepping into Flow

Now that we've begun to explore what this journey might hold...
Let's take a breath.
And step into the rhythm of flow.

Flowcrafting is not about producing polished pieces or following a step-by-step method. It's about something far more intimate — how we *become* in the act of creating.

This kind of creativity doesn't ask you to be skilled. It asks you to be present. It invites you into a space where time loosens its grip, where expectations fall away, and where something quiet and true begins to stir within you.

Flow is not confined to paintbrushes or pages or woven threads. It spills into the everyday — into how we listen, how we breathe, how we see ourselves reflected in the world around us. It whispers to us that there is no one way to move through life, and no single definition of what it means to create.

Throughout this book, you'll find invitations — some offered as reflections, others as questions, and many as moments of creative exploration. You may come across lines that move like whispers or phrases that settle into the space of silence. Some sections flow like poetry. Others feel more like a conversation.

Unspooling the Thread: Starting Exactly Where You Are

You are not expected to follow a straight line.
You are invited to follow what feels alive.

This is not a book of instruction. It is a book of return — a return to your own rhythm, your own way of seeing and becoming. Flow-Inspired Creations are not techniques to master; they are doorways to reconnecting with yourself, as you are, without needing to prove or perform.

Here, there is space for difference.
For softness.
For starting again.

This book is an offering. An open-handed invitation to meet yourself in a new way. To explore what it means to belong — not by trying to fit in, but by letting yourself unfold, moment by moment, into who you already are.

Exploring, Expressing, and Thriving in Your Uniqueness

As you journey through these pages, you'll experience Flow-Inspired Creations — what I sometimes call flowcrafting — in various forms, discovering how creative expression can reshape old narratives, uncover strengths, and foster moments of deep connection. From unstructured play to mindful storytelling, from nature's patterns to the rhythms of sound, this book presents reflections, insights, and practices to help you unveil your unique gifts and discover who you are.

Through this process, you might start to see yourself in a new light — recognising your creativity not as an external performance but a natural expression of your inner flow. You'll discover new ways to engage with your uniqueness, transform self-doubt into curiosity, and step into a space where authenticity and self-expression feel effortless. More than anything, this book is an invitation: to explore, to express, and to trust in the unfolding of your unique creative path, offering your greatest gift to the world.

From My Story to Yours

Before we begin, I want to share a little of what led me here — not because my story holds all the answers, but because it might reflect something of your own.

Uniquely You is a culmination of my life's learnings, blending personal experiences with insights gained along the way. At its heart, this book explores how connecting with your inner flow can shift the feeling of being out of place into a sense of ease with who you are. Flow-Inspired self-expression, empowers you to recognise your inner strengths and embrace the joy of being unapologetically you.

This journey is one I've walked myself, forged through challenges, growth, and transformation. While creativity has been a powerful tool in this process, I've realised that the true pivot point in my life was discovering an inner flow — a state of effortless connection and clarity that allowed me to move beyond make believe and step into a deeper sense of being true to myself. Creativity became the expression of that flow, a means to uncover hidden strengths and embrace possibilities I hadn't imagined.

While I'll share more of my story in the next chapter, *Turning Scars Into Stories*, I want you to know that this book isn't just about my experiences — it's about inspiring you to reimagine your own. Flow-Inspired Creations are at the centre of this book because they offer a pathway to accessing and expressing that inner flow. Whether you're navigating life's transitions, seeking self-expression, or striving to embrace exactly who you are, flowcrafting can support you in moving beyond trying to fit in and embrace the possibility of thriving unapologetically as who you are, by celebrating yourself unconditionally.

Through personal stories, practical exercises, and the transformative power of inner flow, I hope this book serves as a companion on your path of self-discovery. Together, we will explore how Flow-Inspired Creations can deepen your connection to yourself, inspire self-acceptance, and open the door to new possibilities.

Planting What Was Felt

The idea for *Uniquely You* began to take shape about four years ago when, on a whim, I returned to university in search of something different. That decision led me to complete a First-Class Arts Honours degree, during which I wrote an autoethnography as my thesis — a creative and reflective exploration of personal experiences connected to larger cultural and social themes.

Through this process, I began seeing my story in a new light. I realised that the struggles I faced as a child, feeling misunderstood and not quite fitting in, were not unique to me. They were shared by others navigating what it means to be different in a world that often values conformity. Creativity had been my lifeline, weaving resilience and self-discovery into the very fabric of my life.

While writing my thesis, I wasn't consciously thinking about flow, but moments of insights often came unexpectedly, as if guided by something beyond me. A phrase from a radio announcer inspired the title for my thesis. A scene on TV became the seed for a connection I hadn't considered. These small and seemingly unrelated moments felt connected by an unseen thread — what I now recognise as flow-inspired events. They reminded me that creativity isn't just about deliberate effort; it's also about being open to the natural currents of inspiration that arise when we're present and curious.

That realisation inspired Flow-Inspired Creations, a way to engage with creativity as a pathway for self-expression, connection, and transformation. *Uniquely You* is an invitation to connect with your inner self, uncover your strengths, and reimagine your story.

In my book, I invite you to join me on this tide of flowcrafting — a practice not of perfection but of exploration. I hope that as you find your own flow, you will discover the joy of expressing who you are and uncover the strengths and beauty within you.

Listening to What Wanted Expression

Every chapter in this book and each Flow-Inspired Creation exercise is, at its heart, an invitation to connect with yourself,

Unspooling the Thread: Starting Exactly Where You Are

your source, and the flow of life within and around you. These practices nurture a deeper relationship with who you are — beyond expectations, beyond labels. This is the essence of what I've come to call flowcrafting.

When we allow ourselves to enter into this flow, we turn within, creating a bridge to our source — the place where intuition, creativity, and self-awareness naturally arise. This connection is the foundation of every exercise, offering not just a moment of creativity but a means to feel more aligned with yourself and your life.

Have you ever felt utterly absorbed in something, losing track of time as you immersed yourself in the moment? Perhaps you doodled in the margins of a notebook, hummed a melody, or arranged objects simply for the joy of it. That state — where distractions fall away and you feel fully present — is what I refer to as flow — a state often described in creativity and positive psychology alike.

Inner flow[1] is the essence of this state. It's a quiet yet powerful connection to the deeper source within you — a current of clarity, strength, and belonging that inspires creativity and opens the door to new possibilities. Whether it arises while creating art, moving to music, or finding calm in an ordinary moment, flow can emerge both intentionally and spontaneously. Sometimes it's sparked by something simple, like hearing a phrase on the radio or noticing a detail in your surroundings. These moments whisper that flow isn't something you force — it's already within you, waiting to be discovered.

Flow-Inspired Creations invite you to engage with this state more deliberately — to follow curiosity and allow self-expression to arise without pressure. Rather than striving for a polished outcome, it becomes about exploring what feels real and resonant in the moment. Whether through patterns, words, tactile forms, or sound, flowcrafting becomes a way to connect with your true self and express the flow that was always there.

Throughout this book, you will explore how to nurture flow — whether through guided exercises or by embracing spontaneous moments when flow arises naturally. Flow-Inspired Creations focus on what you uncover: a deeper connection to yourself, a moment where curiosity replaces self-doubt, and a glimpse of your inner strength and authenticity waiting to be expressed.

Over time, flowcrafting can transform from occasional experiences into regular practices, bringing clarity, confidence, and joy into your daily life.

> *"When you move in rhythm with your own truth,*
> *life begins to move with you."*
> *— Flow-Inspired Reflection*

The Heart of It: Align, Create, Reframe, Thrive

At the heart of this flowcrafting discovery is a simple yet profound process and motto: *Align. Create. Reframe. Thrive.*

Align

Alignment forms the foundation of everything. It starts with slowing down, pausing, and genuinely being present in the moment. It's a means of connecting with inner flow — the part of us that knows what feels true, even when life feels chaotic or uncertain. You might consider it as aligning yourself with your inner being, your source, or simply a profound sense of presence and resonance.

When we align, we shift our focus inward. We listen — not to the noise of the outside world, but to the quiet wisdom within. This step creates the space for clarity and intention to emerge. In this book, you'll find exercises and practices that I call "centring," which are designed to guide you into this state of alignment with your inner flow.

Create

From this aligned place, creativity flows naturally. Whether through pen, thread, or sound, creativity becomes an expression of your authentic self. It's about the process of letting what's inside flow outward, free from judgment.

Throughout this book, you'll find creative exercises designed to help you engage with this process. These exercises guide you to explore different mediums, tap into intuitive expression, and experiment without the pressure of perfection.

Reframe

Something magical happens when we create from that place; perspectives shift. Through the act of making, we can see our stories in a new light. Challenges that once felt overwhelming may feel less so, or we might uncover hidden strengths and possibilities we didn't know existed. Reframing is about allowing the process of creation to transform how we see ourselves and the world around us.

Thrive

To thrive is to step into the fullness of who we are, no longer held back by the need to fit in or be someone we're not. It's about embracing your path with courage and a sense of well-being, allowing self-expression to lead you toward connection, meaning, and flourishing. Thriving is about engaging with life in a way that fosters fulfilment, resilience, and inner alignment.

When we thrive, challenges become opportunities for growth, strengths unfold, and a sense of purpose deepens. Flowcrafting invites us into this process — not as a destination, but as an ever-evolving way of being — one where curiosity, resilience, and self-belief allow us to show up for life wholeheartedly.

Thriving isn't about reaching a fixed ideal but about embracing who we are — fully and unapologetically. It's about feeling connected, moving forward with courage, and trusting in the flow within to guide us toward growth, joy, and deeper meaning.

When we align, create, and reframe, we step into a new way of being.

The motto — *Align. Create. Reframe. Thrive* — is an invitation to explore, express, and transform through flowcrafting. As you move through this book, you'll discover how each of these steps deepens your connection with yourself, encouraging you to live boldly and unapologetically. It's  about trusting your inner flow, embracing your strengths, and finding joy in the process of becoming fully yourself.

Unfiltered, Genuine, and Whole: Your Authentic Self

When I speak about the "authentic self" in my book, I mean your truest version — unfiltered by societal expectations or the pressure to conform. It's the part of you that feels most aligned, genuine, and at ease. Connecting with this version of yourself is about rediscovering and embracing who you already are, at your core.

This idea is central to *Uniquely You*. The unfolding of this book is about being uniquely you and celebrating it fully. Being exactly who you are without needing to fit into moulds or meet expectations. This way of being means finding freedom, clarity, and joy in self-expression. Through this authenticity, we connect to our inner source and allow our flow to guide us toward unlocking our unique potential.

Flow-Inspired Creations are pathways of discovery — where your actions, choices, and creativity reflect your truest self. By engaging with creativity in ways that resonate with you, you'll uncover insights, strengths, and a sense of belonging that comes from within. This process is about connecting — to yourself, to your unique path, and to the freedom of fully embracing who you are with confidence and easy.

Quiet Trailblazers and Creative Navigators

If you have picked up this book, you are likely just the person it was written for. This book is for Quiet Trailblazers — those who challenge norms and offer fresh perspectives on life's twists and turns, often in subtle yet powerful ways — and

Creative Navigators, individuals ready to chart their own course by transforming personal stories into sources of meaning and strength through creative forms of expression. While these paths may seem distinct, they share common threads of resilience, growth, and the universal desire to belong to something greater than ourselves — a space where you need not try to fit in.

Whether you see yourself in one of these descriptions or seek a deeper connection to your inner flow, this book offers practices to inspire self-expression, explore your unique gifts, and embrace exactly who you are. I hope that it meets you wherever you are on your journey, inviting you to explore the untapped possibilities within and find the courage to be *Uniquely You.*

Your experience with this book is intended to be as unique as you are. Perhaps it's about finding a sense of belonging, discovering clarity amidst life's complexities, creating calm through connection with your inner flow, or expressing yourself in ways you hadn't imagined. Whether through drawing, writing, soundscapes, or another form of flowcrafting, this book invites you to discover your unique approach to thriving. Through Flow-Inspired Creations, you'll learn to express, deepen, and honour this connection.

By embracing flowcrafting as both a tool and a practice, this book offers a framework for uncovering one's strengths, celebrating resilience, and finding joy in being unapologetically oneself.

Belonging: The Courage to Be Exactly Who You Are

> *Belonging begins within —*
> *not in the places that ask us to change,*
> *but in the spaces that let us be who we already are.*
> *– Flow-Inspired Reflection*

These words encapsulate the essence of *Uniquely You*. We have an innate desire to belong to something greater than ourselves — something unconditional, something that doesn't require us to conform or compromise who we truly are.

So many of us have spent years adapting, shape-shifting, or silencing parts of ourselves just to feel accepted. But that kind of belonging comes at a cost — and it's often our authenticity that pays the price.

The aim of *Uniquely You* is to break that cycle. It's about learning to accept ourselves exactly as we are through flowcrafting. When I began to embrace myself fully, I discovered I didn't care as much about what others thought of me. It opened the door to the realisation that I have no control over the behaviour of others — only over my thinking, feeling, and doing.

This shift requires courage — the courage to dare to be different and to be okay with that. It also leads to the realisation that belonging isn't something external; it's something deep within us. It's ours to reach for, and inner flow is one way to connect with it, to know it intimately, and to stand tall in our authenticity.

It's natural to want to belong to someone, something, or a group. But not if it comes at the cost of sacrificing who we are. Belonging, in its truest sense, represents a spiritual connection to our deeper source of being — the same source that links us to everyone and everything in this world. When we connect to that source, the fear of being different diminishes. Belonging transforms into a practice of believing in ourselves and standing authentically in our truth, even if it means being alone — while still feeling deeply connected to our shared humanity.

My hope is that this book provides a glimpse of that connection. Through Flow-Inspired Creations, you'll explore your inner flow and your deepest source of being, expressing yourself authentically in ways that resonate with you. I hope this experience will yield far-reaching, positive consequences in your life. If it does, I'd love to hear your story — please share it on my website.

Turning the Page Within

Our life experiences naturally evolve into stories — narratives we tell ourselves or that others have said about us. These stories hold significant weight, influencing not only how we see our past but how we perceive our present and imagine our future. Yet, while we can't change the facts of the past, we can change the meaning we assign to them. This process of reframing is a powerful act of meaning-making, guided by our emotions, experiences, and the perspective we choose to embrace.

Flow-Inspired Creations offer a pathway for engaging with these stories by shifting our attention to the "gain" — the strengths, insights, and gifts our past experiences have given us. While flowcrafting may not explicitly ask questions like *"Is this story still serving me?"* or *"How might I reimagine it?"* they connect us to a deeper source of our being, guiding us beyond the surface of our narratives to the flow-inspired essence of who we truly are. This process fosters a sense of gratitude for the lessons learnt and resilience for the path ahead, allowing us to recognise the richness in our experiences, even in challenging times, and see how they have contributed to who we are today.

This shift in perspective echoes Dan Sullivan's[2] "gap" and "gain" framework, in which he provides a practical approach to understanding the power of reframing. The "gap" represents what we feel is missing — where we fell short or what we didn't achieve. The "gain," as described by Sullivan, reframes our perspective to focus on how far we've come, what we have learnt, and the strengths we've cultivated along the way. Flow-Inspired Creations amplify this process, guiding us into a flow state where gratitude and resilience naturally emerge. By letting creativity lead, we open ourselves to seeing the beauty in our stories and the possibilities they hold for transformation.

Through this practice, you can begin to see your narrative not as fixed but as fluid and evolving — an ongoing 'artwork' inspired by your creativity, intention, and inner flow. This isn't about ignoring challenges, but honouring them as part of a larger narrative of growth, gratitude, and possibility.

Finding Ourselves Through Stories

Throughout this book, I'll share glimpses of my stories and becoming — not as a complete autobiography, but as threads woven into a tapestry of vulnerability, creativity, inner strength, and the courage to embrace who I am. These stories are not about dwelling on the past but about encouraging you to explore your own narratives. Whether through words, art, music, or movement, your stories hold the power to deepen self-connection and reshape your perspective with intention and creativity. Flow-Inspired Creations offer a pathway for expressing, embracing, and transforming your unique experiences.

Writing about my past wasn't always easy. At times, it was challenging and heart-wrenching, but it also revealed strengths I hadn't clearly seen before. It opened insights that helped me embrace who I am more fully. There were moments I cried — not from sadness, but from release, as I let go of what I had been holding inside. Sometimes, there were tears of gratitude. As it's often said — or perhaps felt more than spoken — 'Tears are the language of the soul, flowing when emotions are too expansive for words.'

Stories — whether yours or mine — hold transformative potential. For the storyteller, they provide healing, empowerment, and a deeper connection to oneself and others. For the listener, they present relatability, hope, and opportunities for new perspectives. By sharing my stories, I hope to inspire your spiral of self-discovery — opening possibilities for honouring and reframing your narrative into something that feels authentic and empowering.

Each chapter offers creative tools to help you connect with your inner flow and express your authentic self through Flow-Inspired Creations — which I also refer to as flowcrafting. These practices are designed to guide you toward fresh perspectives, and they may reveal insights or spark epiphanies that inspire you to navigate your path with authenticity and courage.

How this Book is Structured

Think of this book as your companion, guiding you on an arc that unfolds chapter by chapter. With its combination of storytelling, practical exercises, and creative expressions, it's designed to support you as you connect with your inner flow and discover the possibilities within yourself.

The book opens with two foundational chapters — Prelude: Stories in Verse and Flow and Setting the Stage: Turning Scars into Stories. These are unlike the other chapters in structure and tone. They offer a more personal and poetic beginning, grounding you in the emotional heart of this work. The Prelude is a collection of verses — moments drawn from lived experience — exploring vulnerability, insight, and belonging. It invites you to pause, reflect, and perhaps recognise parts of yourself in these glimpses. In Setting the Stage, I offer a narrative thread that weaves these reflections together, sharing key experiences that influenced both me and the practices of Flow-Inspired Creations.

These early chapters are intended to set the tone, context, and emotional resonance for the rest of the book. While not essential to read first, they create a meaningful foundation for what follows.

All other chapters follow a consistent structure: beginning with personal anecdotes and stories that illustrate the theme, followed by practical exercises and creative snapshots to bring them to life. These exercises are more than just creative prompts — they are invitations to step into flow, that state of deep immersion where time dissolves, creativity unfolds effortlessly, and you feel completely at home in what you're doing. Whether through fibres, sounds, movement, patterns, or any medium that feels authentic to you, these explorations are pathways into the flow — an experience that, once discovered, has the power to spill over into life itself, bringing a sense of presence, fulfilment, and creative possibility beyond the page.

Later in the book, the *Epilogue: Flowcrafting Tomorrow's Stories* serves as a closing reflection — part personal sharing, part invitation. It gathers the threads of this book's evolution and offers them back in rhythm and story. I offer it to you as a space to explore your own unfolding — through creativity, curiosity, or simply the quiet act of becoming.

While you can read this book from start to finish, allowing each chapter to build on the last, you're also welcome to dive into the chapters that resonate most with where you are right now. There are no rigid rules — just an open invitation to explore, play, and embrace your creative flow.

This Is Where We Begin

As you embark on this exploration, *Uniquely You* is here to guide and encourage you. Think of it as a trusted companion, offering support as you unlock your potential, connect with your inner flow, and embrace your uniqueness.

Before we dive more deeply into Flow-Inspired Creations, *"Turning Scars into Stories"* sets the stage — a space where I begin to weave together the threads of my own becoming. It offers a glimpse into how inner flow began to shift my experiences, and how creativity became a path to transformation — a process I've come to call flowcrafting.

Now, let's take that first step into *Setting the Stage*, where story meets self, and flow begins to find its voice — your voice.

Align, Create, Reframe, Thrive

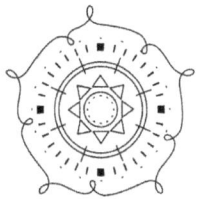

Image 2 **"Uniquely You"** – Collage composed by the author, blending digital elements with creative vision.

Setting the Stage: Turning Scars Into Stories

"We may not get to begin again —
but we can begin differently, from here."

– Flow-Inspired Reflection

Threads of Origin

Through these pages, I hope to say what I once needed to hear: I see you. I see your strengths, your resilience, and your beauty, just as you are. This chapter — this book — is my way of stepping into the light of my own story. It's not always easy to be fully seen, but that's often where scars begin to weave into stories. I hope this invites you to create space for your own.

Every story has an origin, a moment when scattered threads begin to weave into something meaningful. For me, this book's journey began not with a singular event but with the way small moments — insights sparked by music, fleeting images, or quiet realisations — came together like pieces of a larger puzzle. These moments, seemingly disconnected at first, revealed a pattern: the presence of an inner flow.

Looking back, I now understand that my determination to 'prove them wrong' wasn't just defiance — it was a reflection of something deeper, an inner knowing that quietly insisted I was more than their judgments. This discovery became the foundation of my Flow-Inspired Creations, a way to embrace and express the essence of who I am while transforming the narrative of my life. While creativity served as the tool for expressing this flow, it was the flow itself — a connection to something deeper within — that gave me the courage to reimagine my story and the strength to begin anew.

By sharing this chapter, I hope my tide of becoming resonates with you — not in its specifics, but in the connection to the 'why' of my story and the possibilities for healing and thriving. I aim to inspire you to believe that transformation and growth are always within reach. This segment connects the dots between the personal anecdotes shared throughout the book, providing context to my experiences and offering a cohesive view of the process that led me here.

This book is my way of saying, 'I see you.' I see your strength, your resilience, and the beauty of your story — exactly as you are. I know what it's like to feel unseen, but I also know the power of small steps, acts of courage, and reimagining your story. Through Flow-Inspired Creations, I hope to inspire you to uncover your gold — hidden in the cracks of your own pilgrimage.

A Tapestry of Belonging

It's funny how memories resurface when we least expect them. A glimpse of an Airedale Terrier bounding across a field, the reassuring weight of my Swiss pocketknife in my palm, or the distant echo of an *Alphorn*[3] tune can all pull me back to fragments of a childhood that feels like another lifetime. These are the threads of a life stitched together by loss, resilience, and moments of unexpected beauty.

I was born in Switzerland, a land of timeless traditions and picture-postcard mountains. But the life I lived was anything but idyllic. My mother, a brave and determined woman, defied the conventions of the 1950s when she divorced my father. In those days, women had few rights, and divorce carried a stigma that lingered like a shadow over our small family. Her strength and resourcefulness carried us for a few years as she worked and studied to become a midwife. But even her courage couldn't shield me from what came next.

For a time, I lived with my maternal grandparents, who had already raised their own ten children. Their house was a cocoon of safety and love. My grandmother, her hands worn yet steady, would knead dough at the kitchen table, filling the air with the smell of fresh bread. My grandfather, quiet and kind, carved wooden animals for me in the evenings. I loved them fiercely, and their home felt like an anchor in a world that often felt unsteady.

Grossmueti — my grandmother — was the feisty one. She could be loud and fierce when pushed, never one to hide what she felt. But in her toughness, there was also warmth. On birthdays, she would take us to our favourite café in Bern, where the fruit tarts were so fresh, they seemed to hold the taste of the season. Her faith was strong, though personal, and she never imposed it on us.

Like most children, I had my moments. I would jump on my bed when I was excited, even after she had asked me not to — first gently, then with growing frustration. "The lattices are made of wood and can break when you jump," she explained. "I don't have the money to buy a new bed." But at some point, the explanations stopped. The warnings became sharper.

There were other small acts, too — things that must have slowly chipped away at her patience. One day, my little cousin and I were told not to touch the scissors. But I took them anyway and handed them to her, then called out, "Grossmueti, Grossmueti, look, she has the scissors!" She got into trouble, but I was soon found out. I can't say why I did it. I was maybe six at the time. But I remember feeling like she was somehow more wanted than I was — more part of the family. There were things I observed, even if I didn't fully understand them, that made me believe I was different.

Then one day, everything changed. I overheard a conversation through the thin wall of their sitting room — a conversation not meant for my ears. "You need to find another place for her," my grandmother said, her voice edged with weariness. "We just can't manage anymore."

The words hit like a sudden gust of Alpine wind, cold and cutting. I crept back to my room, clutching a carved bird my grandfather had made. I didn't cry — somehow, I already knew what this meant.

Setting the Stage: Turning Scars Into Stories

My mother, doing all she could to build a future for us, simply didn't have the means to keep me. In those days in Switzerland, divorced women had little support, and I — like many children in similar situations — became a ward of the Swiss state.

At eight years old, I was sent to a children's home. The building loomed before me, its grey walls stark against the sky. Inside, the smell of floor polish and unfamiliar food greeted me. An older woman with sharp eyes and a permanent frown stood waiting. "From now on, you will call me *Mother*," she said, her tone leaving no room for arguments. Her voice was as cold as the polished concrete floors beneath my shoes. To my young eyes, she seemed ancient — grey hair scraped into a tight bun, deep lines etched across her face. There was nothing soft about her presence.

I wanted to turn and run, back to the warmth of my grandmother's kitchen or the quiet of my grandfather's workbench. But I didn't. I followed her down a long corridor and into a room where other girls turned to stare.

School became an ordeal. My classmates snickered when I answered questions, my mannerisms marking me as different. "She's odd," they whispered, their words carrying across the room like the sound of shattering glass. The governess — "Mother" — dismissed me outright. "You'll never amount to anything," she said after reviewing my schoolwork one day. Her words etched themselves into my memory, leaving scars I wouldn't recognise until years later.

Years later, when I studied psychology, I learnt about the way trauma can fragment memory. Much of my time at the children's home is a blur — a defensive fog my mind conjured up to protect itself. But certain images remain sharp, like shards of glass in the mist.

One of those shards surfaced years later when I chose to map my family through a genogram. A genogram resembles a family tree but is more dynamic — it charts relationships, emotions, and connections. I resisted the idea for years. How could I map something that felt so fractured, so incomplete? What story would it even tell?

One evening, I sat at my desk, a blank sheet of paper in front of me. "Start anywhere," I whispered to myself, pen hovering over the page. Slowly, hesitantly, I began. Names, dates, dotted lines where solid ones should have been, crossed out lines for broken relationships. And only me in the circle at the end. The gaps stared back at me, a visual reminder of what could have been.

And yet, as I worked, something shifted. The empty spaces no longer felt like failures but invitations. They whispered of possibility, of connections I had yet to make. Donna Haraway's[6] idea of "making kin" came to mind — the idea that kinship isn't confined to biology but extends to all "earthlings." This reframing turned my genogram into something unexpected: a tapestry of belonging, woven not with traditional threads but with creativity, resilience, and connection.

For the first time, I saw my story not as broken but as open — a canvas where I could paint my own patterns. The gaps weren't voids; they were spaces where my creativity and connections could flourish.

Flow, Before I Had a Name for It

Long before I understood what flow was, I felt it. It was effortless, natural — until the outside world made me question it.

The radio played softly in an empty room, and for a moment, the world felt still. The music filled the space, and without thinking, I began to move. My steps had no structure, no form — just an instinct to express, to feel alive in a way that felt uniquely mine. Time seemed to stand still. There was no past, no future; only the music and the rhythm of my body. I was completely immersed in the moment, oblivious to anything beyond the music and the joy it brought.

This was when I was living in the children's home. The feeling of freedom didn't last long. Later, I found out someone had been watching through the window. My sense of liberation became the target of taunts, and what felt joyous to me became a source of ridicule. It was a stark reminder of how different I was — how even the smallest expressions of myself could be judged and dismissed and turned into a story.

Yet, something stirred within me. Each mocking laugh and whispered insult fuelled an inner determination, a quiet voice whispering, "I'll prove them wrong." That voice became my guide, nudging me toward a life beyond the limits others had set for me. Although I struggled in school and was often dismissed, I discovered later that I was holding onto the belief that there was more to me than anyone around could see — though I wasn't aware of this at the time.

Looking back, I realise it wasn't just about dancing — it was a glimpse into something deeper. As if I'd stumbled into a quiet place within myself — a space I didn't know existed. A kind of flow: effortless, instinctive, and true. I didn't have a name for it then, but now I think of it as my inner flow. It's where hidden talents, untold stories, and hopes for who we might become quietly live.

This moment of freedom was fleeting, yet its impact lingered. I didn't have the words for it then, but that feeling — that sense of aliveness — planted a seed. In the pages that follow, I'll share more stories like this — moments that shaped me, challenged me, and ultimately helped me reclaim the parts of myself I once tried to hide.

That experience didn't start my story, but it was one of the first times I felt something stir — something unspoken and alive within me, long before I knew to call it flow. It's a thread that would weave its way into the pages of *Uniquely You*.

The Cracks of Gold

The ache of disconnection defined so much of my early life: the anguish of losing my sense of identity, the silent wounds of trauma, and the suffocating grip of a system that silenced rather than nurtured. Stigma settled over me like a heavy, unshakable cloak. Yet, as I've come to understand, the cracks in our lives — the ones that make us feel scattered, unseen, or not enough — are often where transformation begins.

I'm drawn to the Japanese art of Kintsugi[7], where broken pottery is mended with gold, its fractures not hidden but

Setting the Stage: Turning Scars Into Stories

celebrated. The golden seams transform each piece into something stronger and more beautiful than before. I've come to see my story in this light: a mosaic of fractures that have become golden seams, connecting my past to my present in ways I never expected.

For me, every small step I took toward something better — a little more comfort, a little more possibility — felt like a nudge from something deeper, perhaps even flow itself. This book is, in many ways, an advocacy for those like me who have felt disenfranchised or unseen — a nudge that transformation begins with small, courageous choices. Flowcrafting offers a way to reimagine the narrative, to turn scars into stories of resilience and beauty. Each act of creation becomes an invitation to uncover gold in the cracks of our lives and to see ourselves as whole, even in the midst of imperfection.

Have you ever sensed a deeper nudge — something urging you to take a step toward what feels more fulfilling? A small act of courage, a choice to explore, or a moment of stillness that offered a glimpse of possibility? If so, I hope my experience sparks a sense of recognition — an invitation that your story, too, holds the seeds of transformation. What if the cracks in your story, the ones you might wish to hide, were actually invitations to uncover strength, beauty, and new beginnings?

Let me take you to one of those cracks in my own story — a time that felt fractured and uncertain, but which later revealed itself to hold the gold of resilience and possibility. This is my *Wartheim*.

A Legacy of Resilience

The *Wartheim*[4] Children's Home loomed large in my memory, its formidable stone facade a symbol of authority and isolation. From 1958 to 1965, this institution in Muri bei Bern was my world. It was a place where labels like "asylum for the destitute"[5] and "establishment for correct upbringing" hung heavy in the air — labels that stripped us of individuality and reduced us to problems needing correction.

I didn't end up at *Wartheim* by accident. Swiss guardianship laws at the time wielded immense power over vulnerable families. My mother, a divorced woman in 1960s Switzerland, faced societal judgment and financial hardship with little recourse. Poverty, combined with a lack of government support, left her no choice but to place me under state guardianship.

I still remember walking hand in hand with her through the bustling streets of Bern. Her grip tightened as she tried to hold back tears. "Why are you crying, Mummy?" I asked, looking up at her face. She hesitated before whispering, "Because you don't have a daddy." At eight years old, I didn't fully understand her pain, but her words pierced me in ways I couldn't explain.

My father was a distant figure in my life — there, but not really present. I met him only a handful of times in my whole life, and as a child, I saw him as a stranger more than a parent. It wasn't until adulthood that I glimpsed another side of him — a thinker, a reader, a man with ideals I never had the chance to know growing up. But as a child, I simply learnt to accept what was: that families don't always look the way we expect, and that belonging isn't just about who is present, but about the spaces we create for ourselves.

At *Wartheim*, with the governess, the formality of 'Mother' reigned — distant, stiff, a title worn like armour. We were instructed to address her with the formal *Sie* rather than the familiar *Du*. Her stern demeanour and sharp words were far from nurturing. My grades at school plummeted. "Dumb," the governess called me, and for years, I believed her.

One memory resurfaces like a stubborn splinter. During the time when my mother searched for a suitable place for me, a potential foster family had invited us for a visit. Their home felt warm, filled with laughter, and I played with the children in their yard, imagining what it might be like to live there. But when, later — as an adult — I asked my mother why she had chosen *Wartheim* instead, her answer was simple and heartbreaking: "I thought I would lose you to them." My response, raw and unfiltered, escaped before I could stop it: "Well, you lost me anyway."

It wasn't until much later, while sorting through my mother's papers after her death, that I uncovered the full weight of the Swiss guardianship laws and understood the impossible decisions she faced. Her visits to *Wartheim* became less frequent over the years, and I spent holidays surrounded by girls whose stories mirrored my own — girls with nowhere else to go.

One Christmas, I learnt she had once arrived unannounced to find me sitting alone while the other girls received help with their homework. She later recounted how much it had upset her, but that memory remains blank in my mind, a coping mechanism I've since come to recognise as my way of shielding myself from its sting.

Reframing Kinship

Years later, as I began piecing together these fragments, I discovered a new way of seeing my story. Inspired by Donna Haraway's[6] idea of "making kin," I started to view connection not as something bound by blood but as something expansive and universal. I found kinship in shared humanity, in acts of care, and in the courage to reimagine belonging.

What once carried a sense of void became a tapestry — woven from resilience, creativity, and the profound realisation that kinship can be created, not just inherited. *Wartheim*, with all its scars, became a part of that tapestry. Its legacy, though painful, is also a testament to how far I've come and how much I've grown.

Like the golden seams of Kintsugi[7], the cracks in my life have become symbols of strength. Through Flow-Inspired Creations, I've learnt to transform the fractures into something beautiful. And perhaps, as you reflect on your own story, you'll find your own golden seams — the beginnings of a narrative that is wholly, beautifully, and uniquely yours.

Finding My Voice

The words still echo in my mind: *"Du chasch nüüt, du bisch nüüt, us dir gits nüüt."* ("You are good at nothing, you are nothing, you will amount to nothing.") They weren't just words — they became a shadow I carried for years, shaping how I saw myself and the choices I made.

At some point, defiance took root. If the world saw me as nothing, I would push back. Rebellion became my way of testing boundaries, a silent declaration that I refused to fade into the narrative they'd written for me.

One night, under the cover of darkness, a few of the girls at the home convinced me to sneak out. I still remember the chill of the evening air, the quickened pace of our steps as we hitchhiked into town. We laughed nervously, fuelled by fear and exhilaration. For a few fleeting hours, we were free — until the police found us.

Back at the home, the governess's words were sharp and cutting. I was singled out as the ringleader and threatened with being sent to a stricter institution if I didn't conform. That night, staring at the ceiling of my small dormitory, I made a decision: I would comply; I would keep my head down and do what was expected. But as I made that choice, a part of me went quiet, a numbness that I didn't fully understand at the time.

Lessons from Loss

Amidst the chaos of those years, my grandparents remained a beacon of stability in my early memories. My *Grossvati* (grandfather) had been a kind, steady presence, and though I hadn't seen him in years, his passing hit me with an unexpected force. Sitting alone on the swing in the children's home yard, I looked up at the sky, imagining him watching over me.

"*Grossvati*," I whispered, "if you're there, I promise I'll be better." The swing creaked as I rocked back and forth, the weight of the promise settling in my chest. In that moment, I felt his disappointment — not as judgment, but as a reminder of the values he had instilled in me. It was enough to anchor me, to pull me back from choices that might have led me down a much darker path.

A New Beginning

Despite the struggles of those years, my mother never stopped believing in me. When I turned 16, she somehow managed to enrol me in a two-year sales apprenticeship at Globus, a prestigious department store in Zurich. Around the same time, I was allowed to go and live with her and I was officially released from state guardianship. I still remember the *Vormund's* (legal guardian's) visit to my mother's apartment — his last act of authority over my life. He inspected her unit, ensuring it met all the requirements, speaking to my mother but barely acknowledging me. As he left, he turned to me and said, "The carefree children's years are over now. Real life begins, and it won't be as easy as it has been."

I said nothing, but inside, I knew the truth — those years had been anything but easy. It was striking how he had created his own versions of a story — his, as though my childhood had been protected and carefree, perhaps even thanks to his presence, while I had lived a reality he would never truly see. At that instance, perhaps for the first time, I realised how stories — or the narratives we live by — are created, "written" in our minds, and that they can also be rewritten and reframed. But at that moment his story no longer mattered. What mattered was what lay ahead — the freedom to claim my own path, to move beyond the constraints of guardianship, and to step into a future that was finally mine to create.

I threw myself into the work my apprenticeship required, determined to prove wrong all those voices that had told me I was nothing. By the time I graduated, I had earned third place in the canton — a triumph that felt like reclaiming a part of myself I thought I'd lost.

At 18, the pull of a bigger dream took hold. Australia — my escape, my fresh start — beckoned. With my mother's reluctant blessings, I boarded a plane to Sydney. The enormity of the journey didn't fully sink in until I was alone in a city where I didn't know the language, let alone the customs. But determination drove me forward. Twice a week, I attended English classes, practising relentlessly until I could navigate the world around me.

Eventually, I enrolled at TAFE (a community college) to complete my education, earning my School Certificate and Higher School Certificate. Each milestone felt like a small rebellion against the narrative I'd once believed — that I was incapable, unworthy of success. University followed, where I studied Philosophy, diving deep into Eastern religion and thought — a path that resonated deeply with my search for meaning, connection and inner flow.

Stepping Into the Future

When my mother fell seriously ill, I made the difficult decision to leave my studies incomplete and to return to Switzerland to care for her. By then, I had learnt to see the strength in my scars, to recognise that I was more than the stories others had told about me. Caring for her became an act of reconciliation, a way to honour both her sacrifices and the resilience she had passed on to me.

Her death in 1988 deepened my search for meaning, a quest that had led me to India for the first time in 1979. For 18 years, I divided my time between Geneva and Jodhpur, working alongside a doctor of Ayurvedic and naturopathic medicine, coordinating international conferences. Life as a "jet setter" was thrilling, but it also pushed me to ask, "What truly matters?"

In 1999, I returned to Australia for good, enrolling in postgraduate counselling studies. Imagine coming from where I started to now helping others navigate their own paths toward authenticity and healing. My journey has been a testament to the power of transformation: from a girl who believed she was "nothing" to a woman who has learnt to embrace her story, scars and all.

From Scars to Strength: Threads of Transformation

Looking back, though I might not have been consciously aware of it, inner flow has been the golden thread weaving through every chapter of my life, with creativity as its vivid expression. From sketching raindrops on a page to building a life in a new country, this connection to flow has helped me find meaning and beauty in the cracks — those fractures we so often try to hide. It's this transformative spiral I now offer to you — not as a prescription, but as an invitation to reflect, reframe, and discover your own path.

As you explore your story, you might like to consider these three reflections:

1. **Turning Scars Into Stories of Resilience:** What are the moments in your life that shaped you, even if they seemed like challenges at the time? How might you reimagine these scars as part of a story of strength?

2. **Recognising Your Legacy of Resilience**: What have you learnt from your process so far? You might jot down some reflections in your journal about the strengths and lessons you carry with you.

3. **Finding Your Voice**: What small steps have you already taken to express your authentic self? Are there moments when you've begun to feel your voice emerging?

This isn't about having all the answers — it's about planting seeds for exploration. In the next chapters, we'll dive into more specific exercises and creative practices to help you engage with flowcrafting. For now, these reflections are a starting point, an opportunity to imagine your story not as fixed but as a canvas waiting to be reimagined.

Flow, resilience, and creativity can help you uncover your unique way forward. The cracks in your story, like Kintsugi's golden seams, are not flaws — they are spaces where beauty and strength can emerge. What small steps might you take today to begin weaving a new chapter?

Image 3 **"Turning Scars Into Treasures"** – Collage composed by the author, blending digital elements with creative vision.

The Place I Went to Make Sense

"In flow, we find the quiet path to the more we didn't know we were missing."

— *Flow-Inspired Reflection*

The Birth of "Flow-Inspired Mind Play"

Have you ever found yourself retreating into your thoughts, creating a world of your own — safe, free and fully yours? As a child, I often did just that. I had few friends and spent countless hours alone, sitting on a swing, no matter the weather. In those moments, I would daydream, imagining a life where I could simply be myself — accepted and loved for who I was.

School didn't offer much comfort. It felt like a place designed for everyone but me, a constant reminder that I didn't fit. Teachers and classmates seemed to echo the same message: I wasn't enough. Nature became my refuge — the rain, the trees, even the cows grazing nearby. Unlike people, nature didn't judge me or expect me to be different. It simply existed, offering a companionship that asked nothing in return.

In those moments, something began to take shape. Without realising it, I engaged in what I now call *Flow-Inspired Mind Play* (a form of intuitive, creative daydreaming — open-ended and expressive, not passive or distracting). It wasn't planned or structured — just a kind of mental doodling, where my thoughts wandered freely. Looking back, I see those moments as the beginning of my silent evolution — one that led me into self-discovery. Flow-Inspired Mind Play allowed me to process the world at my own pace, offering a sense of calm and control when life felt overwhelming.

What I didn't know then, and what I'd like to share with you now, is that this practice — this quiet, unstructured way of being — was a form of resilience. It was my way of finding peace when the world felt like it had no place for me. Perhaps, as you read this, you'll recognise moments in your own life when you've done something similar. Those moments, however fleeting, are powerful. They are where creativity begins, where we start to rewrite the stories we've been told about ourselves and begin to see who we truly are.

Opening to Inner Wisdom

Flow-Inspired Mind Play invites us to explore our inner world, where intuitive ideas and creative inspiration can emerge. In these moments, we connect with something deeper — our innermost being — and allow it to guide us. These insights often feel less like something we 'think up' and more like something we 'receive'. By giving ourselves permission to engage in mind play, we open the door to ideas and inspirations that feel authentic and connected to our deepest selves. This process creates a bridge to our innermost being, where intuition and creativity flow freely.

Rewriting Your Story

Our personal stories are formed by the experiences we've lived, the challenges we've faced, and how we've responded to them. But what if parts of those stories no longer reflect who we are or want to become? What if we could rewrite them — reframe how we see ourselves and the world around us?

That's the essence of Flow-Inspired Creations. It's about connecting with your inner flow, expressing your creativity, exploring the stories you tell yourself and reshaping them in ways that align more closely with your truth. Through the mindful, intuitive practice of flowcrafting, you can peel back the layers of your identity, uncovering new insights and crafting a narrative that feels more authentic and empowering.

For me, this journey began with Flow-Inspired Mind Play.

Flow-Inspired Mind Play: A Path to Self-Discovery

Have you ever noticed how your thoughts can take on a life of their own, weaving stories, ideas, and imagined possibilities — almost as if you're shaping the future in your mind? Those moments, when your mind feels free to wander without restriction, can be surprisingly powerful. This isn't the kind of daydreaming that distracts or pulls you away from life — it's a purposeful and creative exploration, a way to connect with yourself and your inner world.

Flow-Inspired Mind Play became a way of stepping inward — not just to process emotions or ideas but to imagine new possibilities. In this space, our conscious mind acts as an observer, watching as thoughts, emotions, and imagined futures emerge from the subconscious. This process can bring clarity, self-compassion, and even moments of profound insight.

Letting thoughts flow freely can reveal patterns we hadn't noticed — insights that offer direction, or even release. These moments can shift our perspective — helping us reframe how we see ourselves or our story. By engaging in this process, we create a space where our conscious intentions meet the deeper narratives within us, opening the door to greater self-awareness and creative possibility.

Flow-Inspired Mind Play invites us to explore our inner world with openness, allowing thoughts, feelings, and ideas to emerge naturally — without any pressure or expectation. It's a way of thinking beyond limitations, expanding possibilities and cultivating well-being through creative exploration. For me, it felt like daydreaming with direction, where my mind could wander freely while also connecting with deeper truths that might have otherwise remained hidden.

This practice became the starting point for my creative expression, offering me the space to pause, listen to my inner voice, and let it guide me. Your process doesn't have to look the same. It's okay to experiment, to try different approaches, and discover what resonates with you. There's no right or wrong way — only the opportunity to connect with yourself in a way that feels meaningful and true.

Whether Flow-Inspired Mind Play is where you begin or something you discover along the way, it's a powerful tool to help you uncover your own truths and start crafting a narrative that feels uniquely yours.

The Space to Think Freely

How often do we let ourselves explore our thoughts without judgment? Do we allow our thoughts to wander freely, noticing how ideas, images, and questions begin to intertwine? This is the essence of *Flow-Inspired Mind Play* — a deeply personal and creative process that grows from moments of introspection. It's more than just idle thought; it's a mental space where we can explore who we are and where we fit in the world.

In these free-flowing states, our imagination comes alive, sparking ideas that feel uniquely ours and opening the door to reimagining the stories we tell ourselves about our lives. By reimagining stories, we aren't just revisiting the past, we're shaping new perspectives, allowing ourselves to see beyond old narratives and step into envisioned possibilities. There's no need to write anything down — unless we want to — or to arrive at conclusions. What matters is the experience itself. In this field of open exploration, we move beyond expectations, where creativity thrives, offering us the freedom to reconnect with our inner world without any pressure.

Flow-Inspired Mind Play also acts as a bridge between our conscious and subconscious minds, allowing us to freely associate ideas and process emotions, experiences, and insights that might otherwise remain hidden. Research on Positive Constructive Daydreaming[8] suggests that this kind of playful, imaginative thinking enhances creativity and problem-solving, helping us uncover fresh perspectives and deeper self-understanding. In this space of open exploration, we move beyond expectations and labels, reconnecting with the person we are at our core.

These reflective moments show us that creativity doesn't always begin with tangible actions; sometimes, it starts with the unfolding of thoughts, revealing insights that deepen our understanding of ourselves and the world around us.

The Silent Origins of Creativity

Flow-Inspired Mind Play often goes unnoticed, yet it's a vital foundation for creativity. It's where the raw materials of our imagination take shape, preparing to surface as inspiration for art, writing, music, or other forms of self-expression. But its true value lies in the freedom it brings to our minds — giving us permission to explore, reflect, and create without constraints.

The next time we find ourselves in a quiet moment, let's allow our minds to wander and notice what surfaces. These moments aren't idle — they're the tender beginnings of creative awakening. By leaning into *Flow-Inspired Mind Play,* we open the door to a state of flow where deeper self-understanding and a stronger connection with our inner world can naturally unfold.

Golden Seams, Bold Stories

You may remember the image I shared in the previous chapter — the Japanese art of Kintsugi, where broken pottery is mended with gold. It's a metaphor that continues to echo through my story, especially in moments where life has felt overwhelming or when challenges have left me feeling different or disconnected. In those times, it's easy to wonder if there's something about us that's "broken." But what if those very challenges are what make us extraordinary?

Kintsugi offers a beautiful way of seeing. The golden seams don't just repair the break — they elevate it, turning each fracture into a feature. What once seemed like damage becomes integral to the new design — one that's stronger, more honest, and uniquely beautiful.

This perspective is woven into flowcrafting. In these practices, there are no mistakes. What might seem quirky, unusual, or different can become an invitation to grow stronger and see opportunities where others see obstacles. Our imperfections are not barriers — they are openings for deeper self-expression.

Kintsugi invites us to cherish the beauty in what feels fractured. Flow-Inspired Creations invite us to do the same, turning perceived flaws into golden threads that connect our experiences and reveal the beauty of our stories.

Inner Reflections, Outer Patterns

What might we uncover about ourselves if we gave our imaginations the opening to wander freely? While Flow-Inspired Mind Play often takes us inward, it also invites us to engage more deeply with the world around us. By creating space for reflection, we begin to notice patterns in nature — grounding, familiar rhythms that mirror our inner lives. The intricate lines of a leaf, the spirals of a seashell, or the ripples of a river can mirror the flow of our thoughts and imagination, offering fresh perspectives on life and our personal narratives.

When we combine this inward exploration with outward observation, such as noticing patterns in nature, we open a dialogue between our imagination and the outer world around us. So often, a thought or possibility takes root in our minds, only to be mirrored in the natural world in unexpected ways. The vast coastline, a pine cone, or a sunflower can mirror our own thoughts and feelings, grounding us while also expanding our sense of possibility. Creativity often begins in these quiet spaces, where inner and outer patterns intertwine.

For me, noticing such patterns sparks a sense of calm and wonder. At times, it feels as if nature is responding to my own reflections, reinforcing what I was already sensing, or offering a new perspective, just when I need it. These moments of connection become doorways into inspiration, revealing that creativity is not separate from life — it is woven into the patterns that surround us. By attuning ourselves to these natural rhythms, we invite fresh insights and new ways of seeing our personal narratives.

Much like *Kintsugi* draws out attention to beauty in imperfection, patterns in nature offer evidence that even what seems chaotic or fragmented holds its own order and grace. Observing these organic designs can nurture our creative flow, grounding us in the present moment while simultaneously opening the mind to possibility.

Looking back, I wish someone had told me that these reflective moments — the daydreams, the unstructured thoughts — held meaning. That they weren't just distractions but valuable openings into creativity. I wish I had known that there's no right or wrong way to explore creativity and that these unassuming moments were the first stirrings of deeper creative expression. Over time, I discovered that attuning myself to patterns in nature nurtured this flow.

Patterns are nature's flowcrafting — the intricate dance of repetition and variation, visible everywhere, from the branching of trees to the shimmer of light on water. As we engage with Flow-Inspired Mind Play, let's notice these patterns. Let's welcome them into our awareness, letting them weave into our thoughts and creative landscape. In their presence, we may find clarity, grounding, and inspiration, guiding us into a state of flow and deeper connection.

Opening the Practice Window

As you begin, know that the goal isn't to create something specific but to notice what naturally surfaces as your thoughts and observations flow. Through this practice, you might uncover new insights, feel a sense of calm, or find inspiration that emerges from the rhythm of your reflections.

Let this be a space of care. If something doesn't feel right, it's okay to step back. It's your call to pause and shape this experience in a way that feels right to you.

Why We Start with Centring

Creativity flows most naturally when we are fully present, grounded, and connected to the moment. In the rush of daily life, our thoughts can scatter, pulling us away from the here and now. Yet, it is in this quiet, mindful space that inspiration takes root, and flowcrafting comes alive.

Before diving into any creative practice, I invite you to slow down and create a space for yourself to simply be. By centring and grounding, we prepare ourselves to notice what is already present — patterns in the world around us and within us, waiting to be seen, felt, and expressed. This practice connects and aligns us with our inner flow, the deeper source of creativity and insight that guides us when we allow it space to emerge.

The exercises in this book begin with centring for a reason: creativity thrives in the present moment. When we ground ourselves, we awaken our awareness, allowing ideas to emerge freely and authentically. Think of this as pressing "pause" on distractions and opening the door to your inner flow.

As we move into this first exercise, let yourself explore without judgment. Let's take a moment together to slow down, centre ourselves, and step into the flow of creativity.

Why We Set an Intention

Setting an intention is a powerful way to focus your energy and bring clarity to your creative practice. Intentions often reflect the "why" behind what we do — they give purpose to our actions and help us stay connected to what truly matters. In each exercise, I invite you to begin by setting an intention. Even a straightforward intention — like 'I want to feel more grounded' — can be enough. This practice not only guides your creative exploration but also becomes a touchstone you can return to, helping you stay aligned with your inner flow and the story only your becoming can tell.

From Observation to Creation

Introduction to the Exercise

Flow-Inspired Mind Play is an invitation to explore your inner world through curiosity and flow. When combined with Pattern Play — observing and reflecting on the patterns around you — it creates a powerful dialogue between your inner thoughts and the outer world. This connection helps ground your creativity in the present moment, offering insights and inspiration that emerge naturally from the flow of both inner and outer observation.

Remember, this is your time and your space. If you ever feel the need to pause, take a moment to reconnect with your intention or simply step away and engage in something different, like a walk, mindful breathing, or listening to calming music. Let this exercise meet you where you are, allowing your creativity to flow naturally and at your own pace.

1. Centre Yourself
- Find a quiet space where you feel comfortable and will not be disturbed. Turn off notifications on your phone.
- Sit in a relaxed position, close your eyes if it feels natural, and take a few deep breaths.
- Focus on your breathing: Inhale deeply, hold for a moment, and exhale slowly. Repeat this three times.
- Let your awareness settle into the present moment. Feel the connection between your

body and the surface beneath you and notice the air around you.

2. Set an Intention
- Once you feel centred, set a simple intention for this practice.
- It could be as broad as *"I am here to explore"* or more specific, like *"I want to reconnect with my creativity today."*
- Let this intention guide your experience.

3. Engage in Guided Flow-Inspired Mind Play
- With your intention in mind, let your thoughts flow naturally while remaining aware of your breathing and the present moment.
- If a specific thought, image, or idea arises, explore it with curiosity. What does it evoke? Does it connect to something meaningful or inspiring?
- If your thoughts begin to feel overwhelming or scattered, take a deep breath and bring your focus back to the intention you've set for yourself. Let this intention anchor you, guiding your exploration with a sense of purpose and safety.
- Remember, this is your moment for calm and creative discovery. There's no need to rush or pressure yourself. Let the flow unfold naturally, and trust the process.

4. Observe the Patterns Around You
- Open your eyes and take a moment to observe your surroundings.

- Reflect on how your Flow-Inspired Mind Play relates to the patterns you see.
- Look for natural patterns, whether indoors or outdoors — leaves on a plant, grains in wood, lines on your hands, or shapes in the clouds.
- Notice textures, shapes, and movements. Are there spirals, ripples, or repeating shapes?
- Can you find a pattern in your surroundings that seems to echo your reflections — offering an affirmation or a new way of seeing?
- Ask yourself: *Can you see a pattern that isn't "perfect" but is beautiful in its own way?* Reflect on how this mirrors the philosophy of Kintsugi — finding beauty in the unexpected or imperfect.

5. Connect With a Specific Pattern
- If a particular pattern catches your attention, pause and spend extra time with it.
- What does this pattern evoke in you — an emotion, memory, creative idea, or sensation?
- Visualise the pattern in your mind's eye and feel its rhythm or flow.

6. Express Your Response
- Translate your experience into a form of creative expression that feels right to you.
- You could hum a tune that captures its rhythm, trace it with your hand in the air, or use an instrument or sound to reflect its flow.
- Alternatively, you can draw it, write about it, or express it through movement.

- Trust your intuition — there's no right or wrong way to explore this.

7. Reflect and Journal (Optional)
- Take a moment to reflect on your experience.
- What stood out to you? Did you discover anything new about yourself or the patterns you observed?
- If you feel inclined, jot down your thoughts in a journal or on your tablet.
- Consider how this exercise might enhance your creative practice or bring fresh insights into your life.

Patterns of Insight

As you wrap up this exercise, take a moment to reflect on the calmness and awareness it has brought to your day. Slowing down and connecting with the world around you opens up space for creative possibilities to blossom. Through Flow-Inspired Mind Play, you've embarked on a path of creativity and self-discovery.

Sharing What Resonates

Did you notice a pattern that resonated with you? Or did you find a new way to express your thoughts? – Your story might inspire someone else.

If you'd like, you can share your experiences and discoveries with others, visit www.flow-inspired-creations.com.au.

Snapshot: A Story of Reconnection

In this blended story, we explore how Flow-Inspired Mind Play can empower someone to embrace their individuality and reconnect with their inner strength. For this narrative, let's call our main character Elena.

Elena often felt a sense of not quite belonging. Growing up, she was drawn to paths less travelled, questioning norms and exploring ideas that others dismissed. While her insights and creativity set her apart, they also made her feel like an outsider. Whether at school, during family gatherings, or later in her career, she felt a lingering pressure to conform to conventional expectations, a pressure that dulled her spark and left her questioning her self-worth.

By her early 40s, Elena found herself at a crossroads. Years of trying to fit into roles that didn't align with her values had left her feeling drained and disconnected. A chance conversation with a mentor introduced her to the idea of Flow-Inspired Mind Play. Her mentor described it as a way to let go of rigid thinking and instead explore the inner landscape of thoughts and feelings through curiosity and creativity. Intrigued, Elena decided to give it a try.

At first, sitting quietly with her thoughts felt unfamiliar. She feared her mind might return only to past mistakes or insecurities. But as she allowed her thoughts to meander without judgment, she began noticing something remarkable. Patterns emerged — not just in her mind but in the world around her. The intricate veins of a leaf, the rhythm of waves at the beach, and even the asymmetry of a cracked teacup began to mirror the richness of her inner reflections. Inspired by the philosophy of Kintsugi, Elena started to see the imperfections in her life not as flaws but as markers of resilience and growth.

Over time, Flow-Inspired Mind Play became a peaceful ritual. During these moments, Elena uncovered themes in her thoughts that helped her understand her struggles and strengths in new ways. What she once saw as shortcomings — her habit of overanalysing, her need for solitude, and her tendency to question norms — now felt like golden seams in her story, threads of individuality that made her life uniquely hers.

One afternoon, while sketching the patterns of a fallen leaf, Elena had a revelation. She realised that her greatest joy came from creative exploration and connecting ideas in unconventional ways. Energised by this clarity, she decided to reshape her life. She transitioned from a corporate role that left her uninspired to a career as a freelance designer, where she could channel her creativity into meaningful projects. The shift wasn't easy, but it felt true to who she was, and with each step, she grew more confident in the authenticity of her path.

Elena's journey with Flow-Inspired Mind Play transformed more than just her career. It gave her the courage to reframe her sense of not fitting in as a gift rather than a burden. Her reflections became a source of strength, affirming that life's most beautiful patterns are often found in the unexpected. Through this practice, she embraced her individuality and began living a life aligned with her values, creativity, and vision.

Closing Thought: Discovery Through Playful and Imaginative Thinking

This chapter introduced Flow-Inspired Mind Play as a gateway to creativity and self-discovery, inviting you to let your thoughts wander freely and explore the patterns within and around you. These patterns — imperfect yet beautiful — echo the philosophy of *Kintsugi*, where what seems broken can become a source of strength and beauty.

Through observing these patterns, you've begun uncovering the golden seams of your story, finding reflections of your inner world and new perspectives to embrace. Flow-Inspired Mind Play offers a space to connect with yourself authentically, fostering mindfulness, creativity, and resilience.

Threads to Carry Forward

1. Your story is yours to shape.
Flow-Inspired Mind Play helps you revisit and reframe your narrative, turning challenges into opportunities for growth and self-acceptance.

2. Creativity begins with presence.
Observing patterns in nature and life nurtures mindfulness and inspires creativity. It shows us the beauty in the unexpected and imperfect.

3. Perfection is not the goal.
The process of Flow-Inspired Creation is where the magic happens. Trust that imperfections can lead to meaningful discoveries.

Every time you pause to reflect, observe, or engage in Flow-Inspired Mind Play, you shape your story — one pattern, one golden seam, at a time. In this unfolding process, the beauty of your true self comes into view.

Image 4 **"Discovering Flow"** – Collage featuring original artworks and digital elements by the author.

When Silence Makes a Sound

*"There are moments when sound carries
what words cannot. A note, a crackle, a breath —
each a messenger of its own."*

— *Flow-Inspired Reflection*

Sound Beneath the Silence

Sound has a way of touching places within us that words alone cannot. A melody can stir a memory, a rhythm can awaken creativity, and even a simple hum can ground us in the present. In this chapter, we'll explore the transformative potential of Flow-Inspired Soundscapes — a practice that invites you to connect with sound in a deeply personal way. Flow-Inspired Soundscapes are intuitive sound explorations — ways of using rhythm, tone, and natural sound to connect with your inner flow. Whether it's the tap of rain on the roof, the chirping of birds, or the resonance of your own voice — sound becomes a mirror to your inner world. It's about tuning in to what resonates within you and allowing that resonance to guide your practice of self-expression and discovery.

Let me share a moment from my own life when sound became both a source of comfort and a catalyst for growth.

Embracing My Sound: A Personal Path to Flow

I was barely fifteen, sitting across from a career advisor with the governess from the children's home looming behind me. The word "Mother" never really fitted. School had been a struggle, and my mark book — a record of my so-called failures — was handed over with the familiar refrain: "Her marks aren't good enough to do anything much."

Those words etched themselves into my mind: "Good for nothing." Tears welled as I sat there, feeling like a lost cause. Yet deep inside, the familiar, quiet defiance stirred once again. The whisper: *There is more to me than you think.*

That defiance grew louder when I worked as an au pair in Geneva. It was a suggestion from the career advisor, a chance to escape the constraints of the home. Geneva became my unexpected beginning. My small room overlooked an office block — not picturesque, but it felt like mine. For the first time, I had space to explore who I was beyond the judgments of others.

In that room, I turned to sound. My mother gave me a small guitar as a welcome gift — an offering of freedom, a bridge between *Wartheim* and the wider world. I didn't know how to play, but that didn't matter. I strummed aimlessly, letting melodies emerge without needing to be "right." It wasn't about getting it right — it was about feeling. The music filled the room and spilled out the window, and for the first time, I felt free.

Later, I learnt this intuitive exploration is often called "noodling." Like doodling with sound, it embraces imperfection and allows creativity to flow. That guitar became my lifeline, a channel for Flow-Inspired Soundscapes. Through those moments, I began to process my emotions, find my voice, and tell a story that felt authentically mine.

Echoes of Culture in Sound

As the years passed, sound continued to evolve with me — shifting from a personal lifeline into a bridge that connected me with a truth larger than myself. It reached far beyond personal healing and into the heart of culture and tradition, especially during my time in India...

In India, sound took on new shape — no longer just mine, but shared, devotional, and steeped in ancient rhythm. It became something I could feel in the bones of a place, and in the voices that carried it forward. Under the strict yet kind guidance of a Marwari[9] musician, I had the privilege of learning traditional chanting — Bhajans and Kirtans[10]. Through this practice, I came to appreciate the rhythms, intonations, and devotion that breathe life into traditions passed on voice to voice.

Looking back, I realise that sound has always been a thread in my life, sometimes personal, sometimes communal, but always transformative. Whether through the unstructured strumming of my childhood guitar or the disciplined practice of Indian chanting, sound has been a bridge — a way to process, connect, and belong. You will read more about culture in *Cultural Currents: Flowing Through Us.*

The Melodies That Move Us

Sound connects us to our creativity in profound ways. Consider how a familiar song can transport you back to a moment in time or stir emotions long buried. Flow-Inspired Soundscapes invite us to perceive sound not merely as background noise but as a language — one that speaks in rhythm, vibration, and resonance, influencing how we feel and move through the world. It's about listening with intention — noticing the pulsing energy of a drumbeat, the hush of wind moving through trees, or the layered voices of a bustling street — and allowing those sounds to provide inspiration for our own creative expressions.

This chapter invites you to explore sound as a medium for self-expression, using it to tap into your inner flow. Whether you hum, strum, or tap along, it's about letting sound guide you into a space of exploration and discovery, where challenges can transform into melodies and self-doubt into rhythms of resilience.

Soundscapes of Self: Crafting New Stories

Sound surrounds us every day, offering countless opportunities for creativity. A distant train whistle, the soft creak of an old wooden floor, the staccato tapping of rain against a window — each carries a story, a rhythm waiting to be heard. Flow-Inspired Soundscapes affirm that creativity isn't about having the "right" tools — it's about tuning into what's already present, deepening our awareness of the world around us.

Sound is more than what we hear — it's an experience that can shift our state of being. A single note can stir emotion, a shifting rhythm can create momentum, and an uplifting melody can guide us into a new way of feeling. Through Flow-Inspired Soundscapes, we can become more aware of how sound affects us and use it intentionally, choosing rhythms, tones, and vibrations that bring us into greater alignment with ourselves. Just as we can select colours in a painting or words in a story, we can tune into sounds that uplift, centre, or inspire us. In this way, sound — like all Flow-Inspired Creations — becomes a tool for reframing, helping us step into a space of possibility, clarity, and ease.

Pay attention to how different sounds make you feel. Some may bring calm or joy, while others might feel unsettling. If a sound doesn't feel comfortable, it's best to pause and explore another acoustic expression that resonates with you. There's no need to push through discomfort — let your feelings guide you toward sounds that create a sense of ease and flow. Let these guideposts nurture both your creativity and inner balance.

Soundscapes often inspire other forms of expression. A rhythm might invite movement, a melody could spark a visual idea, or a sound might lead to a written reflection. Let these connections unfold naturally, allowing sound to guide you toward deeper self-discovery. As you engage with sound and allow it to guide your reflections, you may find new perspectives emerging, perspectives that help you discover new ways of being true to yourself and expressing your authenticity.

Tuning In: Your Practice With Flow-Inspired Soundscapes

Sound has a unique ability to reveal what resonates within you, guiding you toward deeper self-discovery and authentic expression, offering a bridge to your inner world.

Before you begin, take a moment to ground yourself by settling in and setting your intention for this practice. This is your exploration — let it feel safe and meaningful. If any sounds feel unsettling, honour that intuition, discontinue, choose a different sound and reconnect with your intention. There's freedom in knowing that flowcrafting is fluid and adaptable, allowing you to shape the experience to suit your needs.

Exercise: Flowing with Sound

1. **Centre Yourself**
   - **Settle In**: Find a quiet space where you can explore sound without interruptions. Sit comfortably, close your eyes if it feels right, and take a few slow breaths, releasing any tension as you exhale.
   - **Anchor in the Present**: Shift your focus to the sensation of your breath. Feel its rhythm, letting it ground you in the here and now.
   - **Set an Intention**: Reflect on what you'd like to explore — calm, creativity, or connection. This intention will guide your session and help you stay grounded if your thoughts wander. Here are some examples to guide you:

'I intend to find my true voice and express it freely,' or 'I invite these sounds to help me discover what feels authentic and aligned with who I truly am.'

2. Set the Scene
- Gather instruments and objects or simply use your voice. A tambourine, a drum, or even tapping rhythms on a surface can be part of your soundscape.
- If you prefer, play soft, pleasing background music to inspire you. Let it guide your exploration as a companion.

3. Explore Freely
- **Experiment**: Start playing with sounds — hum, tap, strum, or use your voice. Explore without judgment, allowing rhythms and tones to emerge naturally.
- **Notice Your Feelings:** Pay attention to how different sounds affect you. Some may evoke calm or joy, while others might not resonate as well. If a sound feels off or unsettling, take a moment to reconnect with your intention and explore a different sound that feels more aligned with your flow.

4. Discover Your Resonance
- Focus on the sounds that resonate most deeply with you. Allow them to guide you into a deeper connection with your inner flow. As you listen, observe any sensations or inspirations that arise. These moments

can offer insights into your authentic self and how sound connects you to your unique way of being and expressing yourself.

5. Expand Your Expression (Optional)
- Translate your soundscape into another form of creative outlet. Let a rhythm inspire movement, sketch the shapes it evokes, or write a few words that reflect its flow.
- Trust your intuition — there's no wrong way to explore.

6. Reflect and Write (Optional)
- After your session, take a moment to jot down your thoughts, insights, or discoveries. Did a sound resonate deeply with you? Did you uncover a sense of alignment or a feeling of being at home with yourself?
- Journaling can also help you explore sound and create a meaningful story of your experience.

7. Record Your Sounds (Optional)
- Record your soundscape using your phone or another device. These recordings can inspire future sessions or serve as a touchstone for revisiting your practice.

8. Connect and Share (Optional)
- Share your experience with a trusted friend or invite them to join you. This practice can be even more enriching when explored together.

- Sharing is entirely optional — only do so when it feels right and adds value to your process.

9. Embrace the Process
- Return to this practice whenever you feel like it, and seek clarity, creativity, or self-expression. Each session offers a new opportunity to connect with sound.
- Over time, revisit your journal or recordings to celebrate your growth and the insights you've gained.

Rhythms of Discovery

Flow-Inspired Soundscapes invite you to pause, listen, and simply be. In this space of presence, creativity unfolds naturally — not through perfection, but through curiosity. Each hum, beat, or melody becomes a brushstroke on the canvas of your story, a rhythm that brings you closer to yourself. Let this practice be a journey of self-discovery — not about finding the perfect note, but about being present for the music that flows within.

Snapshot: Finding Focus Through Sound

In this blended story, we explore how Flow-Inspired Creation with sound can create a pathway to focus and balance, empowering someone to connect with their unique rhythm. For this story, we'll call our main character Jamie.

Jamie, at twenty-eight, has always felt that the world around him seemed to move just a little too fast. He often finds it challenging to concentrate, with thoughts and emotions pulling his attention in different directions. Daily life can feel overwhelming and staying organised doesn't always come easily. Yet there's one thing that has always helped Jamie feel grounded: sound. Without formal training, he's developed a natural affinity for rhythm. Tapping, drumming, humming — these simple actions have long been his way of channelling restlessness into moments of calm.

As a graphic designer, Jamie faces demanding deadlines and projects that require sustained focus and creativity. Yet the pressures of work often leave him feeling scattered, drained, and frustrated. Traditional mindfulness practices hadn't resonated with him; sitting still and watching his mind felt impossible. He realised he needed a more dynamic outlet — one that would allow him to express and channel his energy rather than simply observing it.

A conversation with a friend introduced Jamie to flowcrafting with sound. This wasn't about learning music through formal lessons or adhering to strict rules. Instead, Flow-Inspired soundscapes invited him to explore sound intuitively — free of judgment or expectation. The idea intrigued him: a creative space where sound could help him connect with himself on his own terms.

With a few simple instruments — a hand drum, a tambourine, and even objects from around his apartment like empty jars and wooden spoons — Jamie began experimenting. He tapped out rhythms, letting the beats flow naturally, exploring how they made him feel. As he added vocalisations like humming or soft clicking sounds, he discovered which tones resonated most. Just ten minutes of this practice each morning became a grounding ritual, helping him start his day with focus and balance.

What began as a morning ritual grew into a rhythm of becoming that anchored his day. Jamie found himself turning to sound in moments of frustration or restlessness, recalibrating before tackling a challenging task. It wasn't about achieving perfect rhythm or creating a polished result; it was about finding clarity and calm in a way that felt both natural and satisfying.

Jamie began recording some of his sessions, curious about how different sounds affected his mood and energy. Patterns emerged: Certain rhythms brought him clarity, while others helped him release pent-up emotions. This newfound awareness gave him a better understanding of his needs and how sound could be a tool for self-care. Whether he needed a soothing rhythm to ground himself or an energising beat to stay motivated, Flow-Inspired soundscapes helped him tune into his own rhythms and intuition.

Over time, this practice became a source of joy and self-discovery for Jamie. Through sound, he found not only focus and grounding but also a deeper sense of self-acceptance. He learnt to embrace his unique energy, using it to create moments of calm and creativity that made daily life more manageable. Flow-Inspired soundscapes became more than a tool — they became a celebration of his ability to find harmony in his own unmistakable rhythm.

Closing Thought: The Soundtrack of Your Story

In this chapter, we explored the transformative power of Flow-Inspired Soundscapes. This practice invites you to connect with sound as a path to self-expression, clarity, and personal transformation. Flowing with sound is about embracing rhythm, tone, and intuitive exploration as tools to step into possibility, clarity, and ease.

Through a personal anecdote and Jamie's story, we saw how sound can help us focus, shift our state of being, and create moments of calm, even amidst life's challenges. The practical steps we covered — centering yourself, experimenting with sound, and reflecting on what resonates — are designed to guide you in finding your own rhythm and flow.

Flow-Inspired Soundscapes invite you to connect with your inner flow and express your authentic self. Each sound becomes a step toward discovering what feels true to you, creating a story that reflects your unique experience and the possibilities within.

Threads to Carry Forward

1. **Playful Exploration:** Flow-Inspired Soundscapes encourage free and intuitive exploration of sound, exploring new ways of being and feeling.

2. **Personal Insight:** By tuning into sounds that resonate with your emotions, you can deepen your self-awareness and connect with your true self.

3. **Reframing Narratives:** Sound offers a pathway to shift old, limiting beliefs and create empowering stories that align with who you are becoming.

4. **Authentic Expression:** This practice is deeply personal, giving you the freedom to experiment and shape your creative expression in ways that feel uniquely yours.

Creativity through Flow-Inspired Soundscapes goes beyond sound or art — it's about rediscovering the beauty of uniquely you. Each time you engage with this practice, you're not just giving voice to old labels — you're reclaiming and celebrating the story that's always been yours.

If this chapter sparked a new thread of understanding for you, I'd love to hear. You're warmly invited to share your reflections or Flow-Inspired Creations at www.flow-inspired-creations.com.au.

Image 5 **"Soundscapes"** – Collage featuring original artworks and digital elements by the author.

When Symbols Speak

"Every symbol holds a thousand meanings.
What it reveals depends on the story we bring to it."

— *Flow-Inspired Reflection*

The Nature of Belief

To me, belief is a thought we keep thinking repeatedly — so often that it becomes a part of our knowing. Though these patterns of thought may feel ingrained, they aren't fixed. Instead, over time, beliefs can shift, responding to growth, fresh perspectives, or unexpected insights. Like branches swaying in the wind or leaves falling in the rain, our thoughts are not static — they are flexible, open to transformation.

When we engage with flowcrafting, we create a space to reach for better-feeling thoughts. Through the flow process, we naturally explore perspectives that nurture curiosity and self-compassion, loosening the grip of old narratives.

This chapter is about belief — the kind that transforms. Belief that can shift quietly, sometimes through unexpected channels — including the language of symbols. It's about finding belief not just in the words of others but in your own ability to see yourself differently. Through the practice of flowcrafting, you may begin to shift the old narratives, embrace your individuality, and explore new ways to express who you truly are.

For me, this shift began with a simple yet meaningful moment that forever changed the way I saw myself.

Raindrops of Change: A New Vision for Myself

Have you ever felt the subtle thrill of discovering something new about yourself — a truth you didn't know was there but had been waiting all along? That's the beauty of flow: it opens doors to parts of ourselves that others might not see and it brings our potential into focus.

At sixteen, I was navigating one of the most significant crossroads of my life: starting a sales apprenticeship at Globus, a renowned department store in Zurich. It wasn't just a job — it was an opportunity to prove that I could carve out a meaningful path beyond the shadow of others' low expectations. Around this time, I met Ruedi[11], my first sweetheart, whose curiosity about the world and zest for learning were infectious. "Have you ever noticed," he'd say, gesturing at an ordinary thing, "how incredible this is when you really think about it?" He had a way of seeing the remarkable in the everyday, and his excitement had a way of drawing me in.

When Symbols Speak

One particular day stands out. We sat in his parents' car as rain drizzled against the windows. "Look at the raindrops," Ruedi said, pointing at the glass. "See how the bigger ones slide down while the smaller ones catch the wind and move unpredictably?" His voice was full of wonder, as if he were describing the secrets of the universe.

I nodded, watching the tiny drops zigzag across the pane. "It's like they have a rhythm of their own," I murmured, half to myself.

That evening, I couldn't shake the image of those raindrops. With a pen in hand, I started to sketch, letting my lines mimic their fluid movements. The page filled with curves and connections, and words began to flow alongside the shapes, creating a message that was playful and alive. It wasn't about perfection or skill — it was about letting myself explore.

When a visiting neighbour later noticed the sketches hanging in my room, they asked, "Did you make these?"

"Yes," I replied, almost shyly. For a moment, I felt the vulnerability of owning my creation — but also a quiet pride.

"Not bad at all," they said, and I couldn't help but smile.

It was Ruedi's encouragement and belief in me that lit the spark. He'd often say, "You're clever — you'll do well," in a tone so certain it was hard not to believe him. It wasn't just about the words he said, though — it was the way he saw me, as someone capable. He instilled a new belief in me. For the first time in my life, I began to glimpse possibilities I hadn't allowed myself to imagine. That's when I had the epiphany that beliefs are just repeated thoughts that can shift and change.

Looking back, those raindrops became more than just a memory. They were the beginning of a new way of seeing myself — not through the lens of what others expected, but through the lens of creativity and possibility. Ruedi's encouragement, those simple words and moments of curiosity had a ripple effect on my life.

Ruedi's dreams were big — he spoke often about Australia, a place where he envisioned a life full of opportunity and growth. "You should come, too," he told me one day, his eyes alight with excitement. Inspired by his confidence, I applied for migration. He left for Australia not long after, and our paths quietly drifted apart. It would take a couple of years for my application to be approved, and in that time, I lost touch with him. But that decision marked the beginning of a journey I never could have foreseen.

Another epiphany came to me much later: *One of the most profound gifts anyone can offer someone is believing in them.* An unwavering belief in their potential can ignite the courage they need to dream bigger, take bold steps, and achieve what once seemed out of reach. In seeing their possibilities, we help them see themselves in a new and empowering light.

Symbols: A Gateway to Self-Discovery

Have you ever felt drawn to a certain shape or pattern, as though it held a quiet meaning just for you? A circle might feel calming, a spiral might whisper of growth, or an everyday object might evoke a memory or emotion you can't quite explain. These symbols might seem ordinary at first, but they often reflect a deeper knowing — echoes of your inner world, waiting to be noticed.

When we engage with symbols by way of flowcrafting, something magical happens. Instead of trying to articulate feelings or thoughts, we let our hands wander freely, letting shapes and patterns emerge spontaneously. It's not about drawing something "perfect." In fact, seeking perfection often distracts from what the symbol is trying to say. These symbols carry a quiet wisdom, offering glimpses of our inner stories — sometimes revealing things we didn't even know we were holding.

As you explore, you might notice a particular shape repeatedly. It could be a spiral, a branching line, or a symbol that feels uniquely yours. What might it be trying to tell you? Symbols can become companions in your becoming, markers that guide you through challenges or celebrate your uniqueness.

In this chapter, we'll delve into how symbols can offer fresh insights and help us connect with parts of ourselves that words can't always reach. Let these symbols become doorways to deeper understanding, inviting you to step into the boundless possibilities of your inner world.

Discovering Strengths Through Creativity

As you have seen, I often felt defined by what I couldn't do growing up — messages about my limitations that turned into beliefs, following me wherever I went. But when I started exploring what I now call Flow-Inspired Creations and flowcrafting, I realised that creativity, when coupled with flow, had a way of offering a shift: freedom. It allowed me to step beyond those limiting beliefs and explore strengths I didn't even know I had. Back in those early 'raindrop days', I did not have the words for what I was doing. The terms "Flow-Inspired Creations" and flowcrafting came much later.

More than making, flowcrafting invites us to see ourselves differently. Each time I picked up a pen or began to draw, I could feel something shifting — like I was claiming a little more of myself. That sense of discovery didn't stay within the lines of my sketches; it flowed into how I approached challenges and saw possibilities, and even how I connected with others.

And it wasn't just me. Over the years, I've seen how flow-inspired creativity kindles a universal thread in all of us — to rediscover hidden parts of ourselves. It's a shared journey, a whisper that we all have the ability to reimagine who we are and to change our beliefs. It's the beginning of believing in ourselves.

Symbols as Tools for Transformation

Symbols are everywhere in our lives — guiding us, inspiring us, and sometimes speaking louder than words. In our daily routines, symbols communicate meaning effortlessly: a red traffic light tells us to stop, while an arrow points us toward a new direction. Beyond these practical cues, other symbols take on deeper, personal meanings. A circle can symbolise continuity, a tree strength, or a butterfly can signal change, growth, hope. Have you ever noticed how certain shapes seem to resonate, almost like they're holding a message meant just for you?

Symbols in Motion

These sample swirling forms speak a language beyond words — evoking movement, transformation, and the rhythm of becoming. They invite not a single meaning, but a space to wonder, to feel, to connect.

You might see cycles, energy, unfolding paths — or something else entirely. Let them be received with openness, the way symbols often arrive: quietly, unexpectedly, and deeply personal.

Swirls in stillness — like questions without question marks. Let them echo gently. There's no need to know.

When Symbols Meet Flow

In Flow-Inspired Creations, symbols become more than just shapes or lines — they transform into a language of self-expression. Flow allows symbols to surface naturally, emerging from the movement of your hand and the openness of your mind. A heart might reflect love; an owl, wisdom or intuition; while a spiral could symbolise growth and transformation.

Flow and symbols are interconnected — both represent pathways, cycles, and unfolding possibilities. Like a flowchart that maps out directions, symbols can serve as abstract guides, inviting us to explore the narratives within us. Their meanings don't have to be immediate. Sometimes, a symbol's significance emerges gradually, like a conversation with your inner self. What stories might your symbols begin to tell? What doors might they open?

> *"A pattern seen through the lens of meaning*
> *becomes a symbol.*
> *It's not what we see—*
> *it's what stirs in us when we do."*
> *— Flow-Inspired Reflection*

Finding Inspiration in the Everyday

Symbols often arrive unexpectedly — from within. But for those unsure where to begin, patterns can offer a starting point. Noticing the repetition, rhythm, or form of something around you might be the doorway into something more.

If you're unsure where to start, let the world around you inspire you. Nature offers patterns full of meaning — cloud formations, the structure of a leaf, or the patterns of waves in the ocean. What do these patterns awaken in you? Could they become symbols of balance, renewal, or connection?

Patterns are the raw materials. Symbols are how we make sense of them. Often, what we first recognise as a pattern becomes a symbol when it stirs a knowing within us.

Even everyday objects hold potential meaning. A pen might represent creativity, a chair rest, or a cup nourishment. These items are part of the visual language of your life. As you draw them, consider what they evoke. What emotions, memories, or meanings do they stir?

There's no need to overthink — just begin. Let your hand move freely and see what emerges. Over time, the patterns you create may take on personal meaning, becoming talismans that reflect your seasons and your strengths.

Bringing Symbols to Life

Engaging with the 'raw material' — patterns — is an invitation to notice how you make meaning. What does the pattern stir in you? What might it symbolise? In this way, working with a pattern to uncover the symbol it holds — often uniquely for you — isn't about immediate understanding; it's about discovery.

Symbols don't give answers — they offer space. Space for interpretation, for curiosity, for subtle revelation. Sometimes they arrive fully formed — an image, an object, a shape that carries something felt but not yet explained. Other times, they evolve from patterns we return to, over and over, until something stirs.

Each time you create or recognise a symbol, you have the potential to reframe a part of your story — whether it's one of resilience, growth, or simply being present in the moment. That moment of connection? That's where meaning meets you. And it's deeply yours.

You can start with a pattern. A swirl, a rhythm, a line repeated. Let it be what it is. If it feels good to draw — on paper or tablet — keep going. If it calms you, stay with it. But notice — if a knowing begins to stir: a thought, a memory, a meaning that starts to surface — that's the moment the pattern becomes a symbol. Not because you planned it, but because it found you. Symbols aren't invented — they emerge. This is how meaning rises in flow.

Symbols within Flow-Inspired Creations become invitations — a way to explore what lies beneath. Each symbol becomes a step toward deeper self-awareness, helping you uncover not just who you are but who you are becoming.

Let's Begin the Practice

Now, let's bring these ideas to life through a practical exercise. You may begin with a pattern — something simple and familiar — but as you stay with it, you may find it shifts. It might begin to carry meaning. It might become a symbol.

Exploring this transformation with curiosity and openness creates a space where your inner flow and self-belief can shine.

1. Centre Yourself
- Find a quiet, comfortable space where you won't be disturbed. If possible, switch off your phone.
- Close your eyes if it feels natural and take a few deep breaths, letting tension melt away as you exhale.
- Focus on the rhythm of your breathing, grounding yourself in the present moment. With each breath, imagine creating a space within you — a space where inner flow can rise, bringing clarity and creativity to the surface.

2. Set an Intention
- Choose a simple intention for this session. It could be "I am open to discovery" or "I will create without judgment."
- Let this intention act as a guide, anchoring you in the flow of your experience. Setting an intention is about bringing awareness to what you wish to focus on, allowing it

to shape your exploration with clarity and purpose.

3. Notice Patterns Around You
- Open your eyes and take in your surroundings. Look for textures, lines, or shapes that catch your attention.
- You might notice the flower petals, the play of light and shadow, or spider webs.
- Trust your intuition to guide you toward a shift that feels significant or meaningful.

4. Begin Creating
- Focus on your paper or tablet and let your observations inspire you. Draw lines, shapes, or patterns based on what you noticed.
- Let your hand move freely, following the rhythm of your thoughts and feelings.
- There's no right or wrong — enjoy the process as it unfolds.

5. Reflect on Your Symbols
- Once you've completed your creation, take a step back and observe it.
- Ask yourself: "What feelings or thoughts does my creation evoke?" How does it connect to my intention or current experience?
- Let these reflections deepen your understanding of yourself and your creative process.

6. Expand Your Expression (Optional)
- If inspired, translate your symbol into another form of creativity. It may spark a piece of writing, movement, or sound.
- Follow where your curiosity leads.

7. Share and Celebrate (Optional)
- If you feel comfortable, share your creation with others — whether through journaling, connecting with a trusted friend, or joining a creative community.
- Celebrate the process and the insights it brought to light, acknowledging the unique expression you've created.
- If you'd like, share your experiences and reflections at www.flow-inspired-creations.com.au.

Snapshot: Symbols of Strength

In this snapshot, we explore how flowcrafting with symbols can reframe someone's narrative. For this blended story, we'll call our main character Maya.

Maya often felt stuck in a cycle of doubt and frustration. Life's challenges sometimes left her feeling disconnected from herself and unsure of her path forward. On the surface, she managed her responsibilities, but inside, she carried a weight that was difficult to put into words.

One day, Maya decided to join a creative workshop. She wasn't sure what to expect but was drawn to the idea of exploring symbols to reflect on her experiences. The facilitator began with a centering exercise, encouraging the participants to let go of judgment and focus on the present moment. For Maya, this simple act of breathing deeply and tuning into herself felt unexpectedly grounding.

During the session, Maya was invited to create symbols that resonated with her. She started with a spiral, which seemed to reflect her recurring thoughts and emotions. The spiral grew outward as she worked, transforming into an intricate pattern. To her surprise, it felt like a map of her internal world — complex but connected, with threads leading in new directions.

Later, Maya found herself drawing a sun peeking through a mountain range. It wasn't planned, but as the image emerged, it seemed to represent a quiet hope rising within her. The mountain, once an obstacle, now felt like a challenge she could face with renewed strength. The sun became a symbol of the light she was rediscovering.

Through these creations, Maya began to see her story differently. The symbols offered her a way to externalise feelings she had struggled to verbalise. Over time, the practice became a way of finding clarity and reconnecting with herself. Each new symbol became a small step toward understanding and embracing her journey.

What started as a creative exercise began to ripple into her daily life. She noticed a growing sense of confidence and calm as she faced challenges with the same openness she brought to her creations. The symbols weren't just drawings anymore

— they became touchstones, echoes of her strength and the light she carried within. For Maya, Flow-Inspired Creations with symbols became a way to not only reframe her story but to live it with greater intention and authenticity.

Closing Thought: Unlocking Self-Awareness Through Symbols

In this chapter, we've explored how symbols we've long known can take on new meaning through flowcrafting. They can become a gateway to deeper self-awareness, self-belief, and creative expression. Symbols have the unique power to capture emotions and experiences that can feel too complex for words. They offer a language of their own, one that speaks to our shared humanity while also holding deeply personal meanings that resonate with our individual seasons.

By connecting with the symbols around us — whether in nature, daily objects, or the patterns that speak to us — we begin a dialogue. One between our inner and outer worlds. These practices foster a sense of curiosity and openness so that symbols can serve as mirrors, reflecting deeper meanings that allow us to reimagine challenges — not as obstacles, but as openings for growth and transformation.

Flow-Inspired Creations bring this process to life, guiding us toward self-discovery. Each symbol becomes a gateway toward reconnecting with our inner flow, an affirmation of the strength, clarity, and potential we carry within. As we engage with symbols, we're not just creating; we're forging a deeper connection to who we are and imagining what's possible.

Threads to Carry Forward

1. **Reframe Your Story Through Symbols:** Symbols have the power to help us reframe our stories, deepen our understanding, and uncover new paths to resilience. Each creation becomes a step toward seeing your story with fresh eyes.

2. **Discover Your Inner Symbols:** Every symbol you create reflects a personal truth or insight. Let your intuition guide you as meanings emerge naturally, revealing deeper layers of self-awareness.

3. **Find Inspiration in Everyday Patterns:** Patterns in nature and daily life can serve as seeds for meaningful self-expression, creating a bridge between your external world and inner landscape.

4. **Embrace the Flow of Symbolic Creation:** This practice is about connecting with your authentic self and exploring new perspectives with curiosity and openness.

Flowcrafting with symbols can uncover a language for your inner truths. Let each one lead you toward self-discovery and deeper connection with yourself.

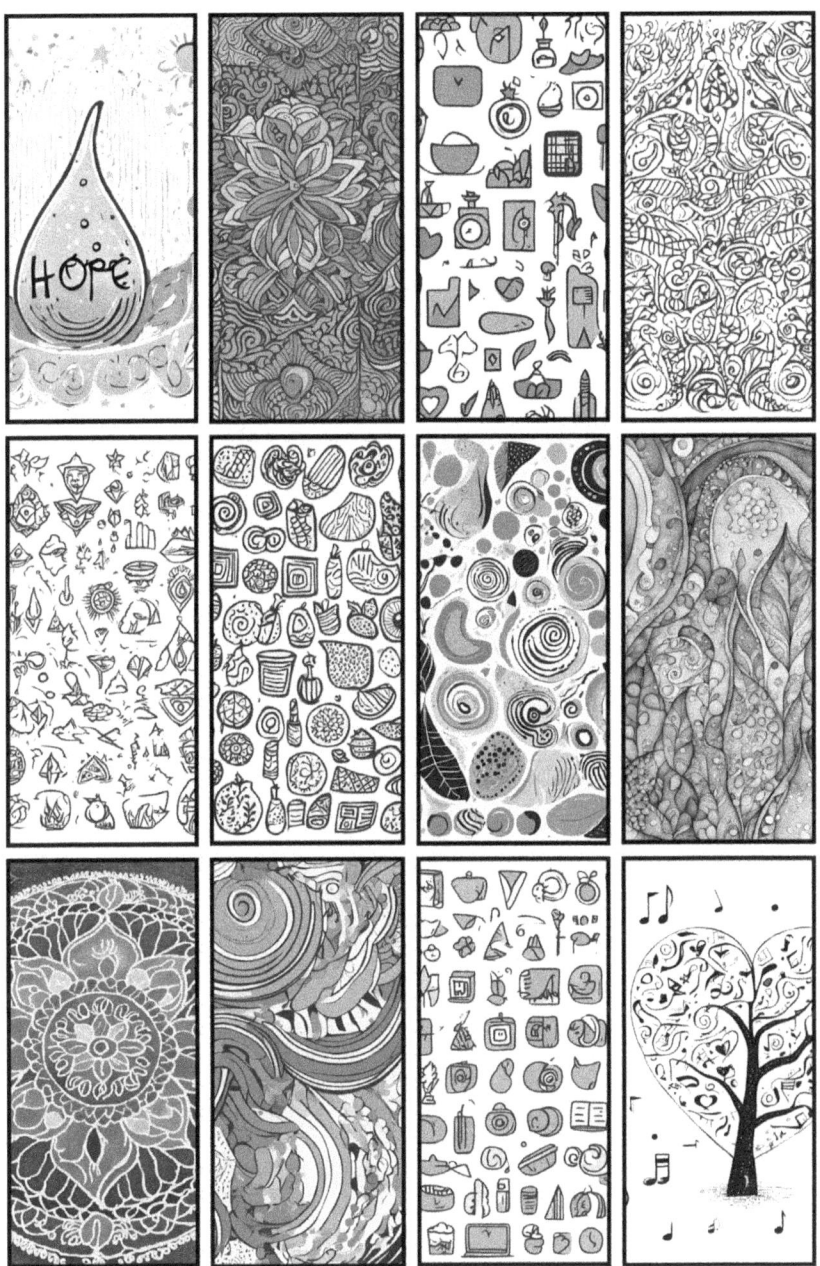

Image 6 **"Bringing Symbols to Life"** – Collage featuring original artworks and digital elements by the author.

Becoming in the Not-Yet-Known

"Flow is the space where pressure fades and presence returns — where we meet ourselves without needing to prove anything."

– Flow-Inspired Reflection

Leaning into Creative Freedom: Dreamscapes

There is magic in letting go of the need to follow the lines — allowing creativity to move freely without expectation or constraint. This chapter invites you to explore that freedom, embracing the flow of creativity, and the joy of self-expression.

Unstructured Flow-Inspired Creations, or what I've come to call dreamscapes, are about letting go.

As I shared previously, I felt an urgent need to rise above early messages of inadequacy — the ones that told me I wasn't enough. Over the years, bit by bit, I began to realise that how I relate to those stories changes how they shape me. Through positive psychology and the discovery of flow, I found language for a sense of freedom I'd longed for — and later, a way to express it with ink. That's how dreamscapes became a celebration of spontaneity — a playground where my creativity could roam free.

I still remember the first time I permitted myself to create like this. I dipped a dropper into the ink and let a single drop fall onto Yupo paper. Watching the ink spread unpredictably, I felt a mix of curiosity and trepidation. "What if it doesn't look good?" a familiar voice whispered. But another part of me — quieter but insistent — nudged me forward: *Just let it happen.*

As the ink spread, I let another drop in a complementary colour fall onto the page. I found myself captivated. Colours merged, bloomed, and shapes appeared — some jagged, others soft and fluid. It was as if the ink was speaking its own language, a dialogue between what was inside me and what was emerging. It was freeing — and surprisingly fun.

I invite you to explore dreamscapes in whatever way feels natural. Whether you use ink, watercolours, or digital tools, there's no wrong way to create. Let your medium guide you. Along the way, you might discover not only new forms of expression but new ways of seeing yourself — free from constraints, full of possibility.

Nothing is fixed in concrete. Even long-held beliefs can shift. I've lived that truth — having once absorbed messages that dimmed my light, only to uncover new ways of being. If even one dreamscape, one moment in this book, reminds you that change is possible, it will have done its work.

Sometimes the most powerful shifts begin with a pause — a moment of openness. A colour that flows in an unexpected direction.

Allowing and Becoming: Embracing Freedom Through Flow

You probably know the feeling of being swept along by life's currents — uncertain of where they're taking you. I've been there, and those moments have taught me the most about myself.

But I wasn't always able to let go. Messages I'd absorbed early on — of not measuring up, of being somehow not enough — had lodged deep. They told me that self-expression was risky, or pointless, or indulgent. And for a long time, I believed them. So even though I longed for freedom, I didn't know how to allow it.

The first time I glimpsed the ache of that truth, I was thirteen. My father — whom I barely knew — made a rare visit to the children's home. He handed me Franz Kafka's *Metamorphosis*. "You'll like this," he said with a faint smile. I didn't understand everything, but the story left a lasting impression. The protagonist's transformation spoke to something raw inside me — an aching question of who I was becoming and whether I'd have any say in it.

That moment sparked an unconscious inquiry, one I now realise stayed with me for years. I began to wonder: could transformation emerge — not from effort alone, but from allowing?

Room for Beauty in Uncertainty

Years later, sitting in a conference on neuroplasticity with Dr Dan Siegel[12], I felt that question finally begin to shift. As I remember, he explained that the brain isn't fixed — that it's shaped by where we place our attention. His words landed like a revelation. My past wasn't a trap, but a starting point. What once felt like inadequacy wasn't the end — it was the beginning of what could come next.

I brought this discovery into my creative practice, exploring alcohol inks on Yupo paper. How the ink moved whimsically became a metaphor for what I was learning. The swirls and splashes weren't to be controlled, but to be witnessed — to be collaborated with.

When the ink dried, I'd trace over the shapes with gel pens, adding layers of detail. Each piece felt like a map of feelings, memories, and untapped potential. I wasn't erasing the chaos; I was building on it, finding beauty in its capriciousness.

It reminded me of something else Dr Siegel spoke about. As I recall, he said, 'Growth isn't linear — it's about staying open to what's possible.'

Free-flow creations became the inner terrain I was learning to walk without a map. Just as the ink found its path, I learnt to trust that my life would do the same. Each creation was a subtle triumph — an acknowledgement that even in uncertainty, there is room for beauty, for freedom, and for becoming.

Finding Joy in Unpredictability

Unstructured Flow-Inspired Creations invite us to step away from the pressures of expectation and perfection, immersing ourselves in the flow of the present moment. This state of flow, where time seems to dissolve and our awareness merges with creating, connects us more deeply to our inner experience. It speaks to the idea that the process itself — the unfolding of creativity — can be just as meaningful, if not more so, than the outcome.

Beginning with a simple intention can help ease us into this state of flow. Your intention can be simple — like 'I am open to discovery' or 'I will create without judgment'. This grounding focus allows creativity to flow naturally without pressure or expectation, creating a space where inspiration can emerge.

Image 15 **"Unmapped – Dreamscape"** – by the author (original artwork, now in a private collection)

As we shift our attention from what we're making to how we're making it, we tap into the richness of unpredictability. Each swirl of ink or splash of paint reflects the dynamic nature of life itself, echoing its unexpected twists and turns. These moments of creative surrender show us a way to find beauty in the unplanned, resilience in the unknown, and adaptability in the face of change. Flowcrafting may begin as a creative practice, but over time, it becomes a pathway — one that deepens trust in ourselves and the subtle current of flow we carry within.

Life rarely moves in straight lines, and this practice mirrors that truth. Unstructured flowcrafting invites us to stay open to the unexpected, discovering opportunities for insight and growth in moments of unpredictability. It helps us find a rhythm and creativity that fosters both calm and focus, gently drawing us into the flow of the present moment.

With this mindset, each moment of creating becomes more than just an activity. It becomes an invitation to explore, reflect, and connect more deeply with our inner flow. As we prepare to dive in, let's be guided by curiosity, intuition, and a willingness to let creativity lead the way.

Exercise: Approaches for Free-Flow Expression

Before starting your dreamscapes, keep in mind: this practice is about letting your creativity flow freely. Approach it with curiosity and playfulness, allowing yourself to explore without judgment. There's no right or wrong here, only your unique practice.

Preparations for Your Free-Flow Session

1. Prepare Your Space and Materials

Before starting your session, take some time to set the stage for creative flow:

- **Create a Safe and Comfortable Environment**:
    - Ensure your workspace is well-ventilated, especially if using alcohol inks. If needed, wear a mask to protect yourself.
    - Opt for watercolours or acrylic inks if you're sensitive to strong odours or vapours.
    - Make the space inviting with adequate but soft lighting and, if you like, calming background music.

- **Gather Your Materials**:
    - Choose your flow medium: alcohol or acrylic inks, watercolours, or other options (tablet & stylus work too).

- Have surfaces or paper suited to your medium, e.g. non-porous Yupo paper for alcohol inks or watercolour paper for wet media.
- Consider additional tools:
  - **Natural Tools**: Sticks, twigs, or feathers for organic textures.
  - **Drinking Straws**: To blow and direct fluid media.
  - **Hair Dryers**: On the lowest setting to move the paint dynamically.
  - **Palette Knives or Scrapers**: For bold strokes and lines.

2. Centre Yourself

- Grounding yourself, as in earlier exercises, helps create space for creativity to move naturally through you.
- Find a quiet, distraction-free space and close your eyes if it feels natural.
- Take deep breaths, letting tension melt away with each exhale.
- Focus on the rhythm of your breathing, bringing your attention fully into the present moment.

3. Set an Intention

- Anchor your session with a guiding thought:
- Reflect on what you'd like to experience. Choose an intention that feels authentic to you. It could be discovery, relaxation, or simply the joy of creating.
- Let your intention guide you throughout the session, providing focus and meaning to your free-flow creating process.

- Let this intention act as your compass, returning to it whenever your thoughts wander.

4. Experiment with Tools and Techniques

Now begin exploring your chosen medium:

Play with Techniques:

- **Layering Colours:**
    - Apply one colour, let it dry or settle, and then layer another. Watch the interaction of hues and textures.
    (Note: With alcohol inks, layering happens wet-on-wet, while the surface is still active. Water-based paints, on the other hand, may require drying between layers — yours to experiment.)

    - **Blending with Water**: In water-based media, use brushes, droppers, or spray bottles to create transitions and gradients.
    If you're working with alcohol inks, blending happens through isopropyl alcohol or blending solution—not water—creating fluid, organic movement.

    - **Letting the Medium Lead**: Release control and allow the paint or ink to move naturally, making room for patterns to emerge on their own.

- **Try Unique Tools**:
    - Experiment playfully with natural materials or unconventional items like drinking straws and hair dryers to create surprising effects.
- As colours blend and forms emerge, this process does more than create a visual image — it shifts attention toward what is unfolding within you. Each stroke, each movement, becomes an act of stepping into what is possible.
- **Add Details (Optional)**: Use markers, gel pens, or brushes to enhance areas that draw your attention.

5. Reflect and Embrace the Outcome

After completing your creation, take a moment to connect with it:

Observe Your Work:

- Did this process mirror something in your own life — where things come together, unravel, or find new connections?

- What feelings, thoughts, or memories does it evoke?

6. Celebrate and Share

- **Celebrate the Process**:
    - Appreciate the freedom and creativity you embraced.
    - Hold gratitude for the insights and calm the process brought you.

- **Share Your Insight**:
    - Consider sharing your creation in a journal, with a trusted friend, or on a community forum.
    - Let others see the beauty of your unique exploration.

A Final Thought

Each free-flow creation reflects your willingness to explore uncertainty. It's about trusting your intuition and embracing the joy of discovery.

Your insights, reflections, and creations matter. If this chapter stirred something in you, you might feel called to connect with like-minded friends and share your insights.

Guidance

If you'd like to explore further, you'll find a wealth of resources online — including tutorials, videos, and creative communities — especially around alcohol inks, dreamscapes, and other flow-based mediums. Let your curiosity lead the way.

For now, may your path of becoming continue to unfold, guided by curiosity, your own rhythm, and the quiet power of flow; each creation, no matter how small, reminding you that you're already enough — and always becoming.

Snapshot: Finding Calm Through Free-Flow

In this blended story, we explore how unstructured Flow-Inspired Creations can offer moments of peace and renewal, empowering someone to reconnect with their deeper sense of being. For this narrative, we'll call the main character Leah.

Leah, a thoughtful and introspective woman in her early thirties, often felt the weight of her busy, demanding life pressing down on her. Between a high-pressure job and managing her household, she rarely had time to pause and consider her own needs. The constant demands of her day left her feeling disconnected from herself, as if she were running on autopilot. Though she managed to stay on top of everything outwardly, inwardly, she often felt overwhelmed and unsure how to break free from the cycle.

One evening, Leah attended a creative workshop hosted by a community group. The facilitator introduced unstructured flowcrafting as a meditative practice — a way to explore creativity without judgment or expectation. "This isn't about making perfect art," the facilitator explained. "It's about letting yourself play, letting go, and seeing what emerges." Intrigued but hesitant, Leah decided to give it a try. Though she hadn't picked up a brush since school, the idea of simply letting the ink flow sounded like a welcome break from her structured routines.

At the start of her first session, Leah set an intention: to let her mind unwind. She chose a palette of soft greens and blues, dipping her brush into acrylic inks and letting the colours flow across the paper. As the inks spread and blended, they formed unpredictable shapes and gradients. Leah allowed the pigments to flow freely, occasionally tilting the paper to see how the colours moved, their paths forming organic, fluid patterns. She resisted the urge to "fix" anything or make it look a certain way, instead allowing her brush and intuition to lead.

As the session continued, Leah noticed something remarkable. Her mind, which had been racing with tasks and deadlines, began to quiet. Each swirl of colour seemed to mirror her own emotions — shifting, softening, finding balance. She felt truly present in the moment for the first time in weeks. The vibrant shapes on the page didn't just reflect her creativity; they felt like parts of herself returning home, fragments she hadn't realised she had been missing.

When Leah's session ended, she sat back to observe her creation. The organic forms reminded her of flowing rivers, a symbol of movement and renewal. She found herself reflecting on how she had been approaching life — always trying to control the current rather than letting it guide her. The thought was both humbling and freeing.

Encouraged by this experience, Leah began incorporating Flow-Inspired dreamscapes into her weekly routine. On particularly stressful days, she turned to her inks and paper, letting the process of creating become a form of release. Over time, she noticed a shift — not only in how she managed stress but also in how she approached life. Flowcrafting helped her embrace the unpredictability of the everyday, finding strength in letting go of perfection and connecting with the flow of the moment.

Leah's story offers a glimpse into how Flow-Inspired dreamscapes can be powerful tools for renewal and self-connection. Through unstructured creations, she found a way to quiet the chaos, rediscover a sense of calm, and reconnect with the strength that had been there all along.

Closing Thought: Flowing Beyond Constraints

In this chapter, we explored the liberating power of unstructured Flow-Inspired Creation, a practice that transforms uncertainty and unpredictability into opportunities for self-discovery. Through my personal stories of embracing ink and watercolour dreamscapes and Leah's snapshot story, we've seen how letting go of control invites creativity to unfold naturally. These stories speak to the idea that flowcrafting in free-flow lies in the freedom to lean into the process.

Threads to Carry Forward

1. **Trust the Process**
   As my story illustrated, creativity flows naturally when we let go of rigid expectations. Trust that each step — whether in art or life — has value, even if the outcome isn't yet clear.

2. **Release Control**
   Like Leah, embracing the unpredictable can lead to surprising insights. Allow your chosen medium to guide you, and enjoy the unfolding patterns, colours, and shapes as they emerge.

3. **Discover Inner Wisdom**
   Your personal stories and creations reflect the freedom, resilience, and potential within you. These moments of flow are invitations to pause, connect with your inner world, and reimagine your possibilities.

As you continue your flowcrafting experience, let it be an unspoken knowing that each creation reflects your courage to explore and express. Whether it's a swirl of colour, a pattern that surprises you, or an emotion brought to life, your creations are milestones on your path of growth and self-connection.

Celebrate the discoveries, embrace the flow, and let unstructured flowcrafting serve as both a mirror and a guide, inviting joy.

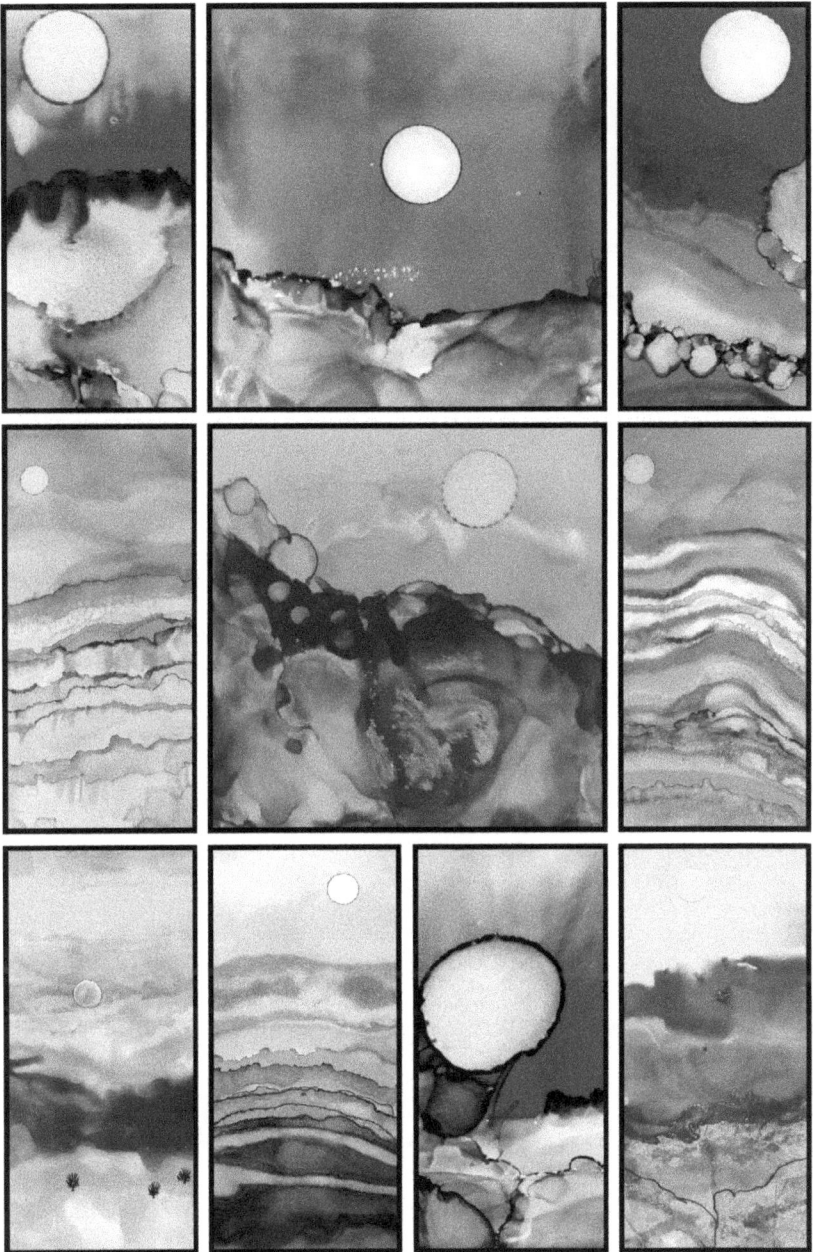

Image 7 **"Allowing and Becoming – Dreamscapes"** – Artworks by the author

Weaving Life's Threads

*" We are the weavers of our becoming —
each thread a moment held,
each choice a delicate stitch
in the story only we can tell."*

– Flow-Inspired Reflection

Fibres of Identity: Crafting Stories in the Weave

Your life is a tapestry, woven from experiences, choices, and stories only you can tell. Each thread holds a moment — some vibrant, some frayed, all essential to the whole. In this chapter, we step into the world of weaving as a form of Flow-Inspired Creations — a practice that goes beyond working with fibres, inviting us to reimagine and rewrite our life stories, one thread at a time.

Weaving is a process of discovery. Sheila Hicks[13], a renowned fibre artist, describes her work as "intelligent play," a practice that unfolds with each thread, much like life itself. With every pass of the yarn, patterns emerge, mirroring the flow of our daily existence — layered, evolving, and beautifully imperfect.

Each thread you weave tells a story. The textures, colours, and materials you choose represent your hopes, challenges, and transformations. The strength of a thread doesn't lie in one continuous fibre, but in how many fibres intertwine and support each other — just as our experiences intertwine to create the fabric of our lives. What patterns are you weaving in your life? What story is unfolding in your hands?

Throughout history, weaving has been a way to express personal and cultural narratives. Woven cloth reflects traditions, values, and beliefs, yet no two creations are exactly the same. In the same way, your weaving becomes uniquely yours — an extension of your inner world.

Discovering Your Story in the Weave

Weaving is slow and rhythmic, inviting you to reflect as the pattern reveals itself, thread by thread. It's a practice of patience and presence, where even the smallest choice — a strand of colour or a shift in texture — becomes a moment of self-expression.

There are no rules here. Found materials, recycled fibres, or natural elements like branches can become part of your creation, encouraging spontaneity and freedom. Letting go of set expectations allows an unexpected shift to emerge — a knowing that speaks to your heart.

If life feels tangled or chaotic, weaving offers a chance to make sense of it. Each thread, even the ones that feel rough or mismatched, has a place in the larger fabric. Lean into imperfections as part of the beauty. As you weave, you might find clarity — an unspoken reassurance that even in the messiness of life, a rhythm and meaning are waiting to emerge.

So, as you begin this exploration, let weaving be more than a craft. Let it be a space to reflect, experiment, and discover the stories within you — offering a chance to create an item uniquely yours, thread by thread.

Resilient Threads: Weaving My Life Narrative

You might be wondering, why weaving? Why do I see it as a form of Flow-Inspired Creations? For me, weaving is a way to explore, express, and reconnect with myself. The tactile nature of fibres — the way they engage both hands and mind in a still, meditative rhythm — makes weaving feel deeply personal. It has become a powerful tool for reshaping my life narrative, helping me uncover strengths I didn't always know I had.

When I was a child, I loved working with my hands. I'd twirl threads, tie knots, and experiment with crochet and knitting. But I rarely finished big projects like knitting a jumper or sewing a dress — I didn't have the patience. Instead, I found joy in the small moments: the feel of the yarn, the motion of tying knots. Yet, even those small joys were sometimes overshadowed. I can still hear my needlework teacher's sharp voice reciting a rhyme that stung deeply: *"Langes Fädchen, dummes Mädchen"* — 'long thread, dumb girl.' It wasn't until much later that I learnt the original saying was actually, "*Langes Fädchen, faules Mädchen*" — 'long thread, lazy girl.' When I found out, I was taken aback. I had no idea she had adapted it, and the realisation made her words feel even more personal.

Looking back, I can see how much those words affected me, but they didn't define me. Rediscovering my love for fibres and weaving later in life gave me a way to reclaim the joy and self-expression that I thought I'd lost. I share this memory because I know that some of you may have been given labels that never truly reflected who you are — words that distorted your perception of yourself but were never yours to carry. It's a vulnerable part of my story, but one that echoes — and I hope affirms for you — that such experiences don't have to define us. We can reclaim the joy and self-expression that might feel out of reach.

At the time, I couldn't understand why I became the target of such unkindness. Why was I given labels that diminished me rather than encouraging who I truly could become? Later, I realised that as a child under the Swiss guardianship law, I had no rights, no voice. I was often treated as though I didn't matter — a 'nobody.' Small moments like my teacher's words chipped away at my love for the crafts I enjoyed, making creative expression feel out of reach.

And yet, looking back, it's striking how even in an environment influenced by control, criticism, and lack of belonging, a deeper thread remained untouched. Despite it all, the direction of a life can change — not by rewriting the past, but by shifting where we place our attention. The simple act of turning toward what nourishes, what uplifts, what feels quietly true, holds more power than we often realise.

It wasn't until years later that I rediscovered the joy of working with fibres. As I wove threads over and under the warp, I saw that weaving wasn't just about creating a beautiful design — it was storytelling. Each thread became a part of the bigger picture, a piece of my story. Like life, weaving is often uneven and imperfect, but that's where its beauty lies. Smooth and knotted, warp and weft — all come together to form the fabric, much like our experiences give rise to who we are becoming.

Now, I see life itself as a weave. Each thread — every choice, memory, and challenge — intertwines with our creative expressions, forming something resilient and transformative. Weaving has taught me that life's narrative can always be reshaped, reimagined, and appreciated in a new light.

I've also learnt to notice the fibres surrounding us in everyday life — the clothes we wear, the tarp on a building site, the grasses swaying in a field — unassuming, steady threads that remind me of the rhythm of weaving and of life. Every choice I make — whether in materials or in moments — alters the texture of the fabric I'm creating... in weaving, and in life.

Some of my weavings hold particular meanings. *Kindred*, for example, embodies my connection to different cultures, a love that's been with me since childhood. Combining tree pods, clay medallions, and dreadlock-like plaits, it became a nature-inspired diary of my process, marking my fascination with artisanal crafts and traditional costumes.

Another piece, *Two Roads Diverged in a Wood*, was inspired by Robert Frost's famous poem. Using a forked branch as the frame, I wove natural fibres, with a crystal at the centre and a stained-glass pendant suspended below. This symbolises the choices we make in life — the forks in the road where we must decide our path.

For me, this piece tells a story of resilience: finding beauty in life's challenges and growth in its uncertainties. The imagery of the forked branch reflects the essence of standing at a crossroad and choosing a path that may feel unfamiliar or quietly unconventional. The title, drawn from Frost's poem *The Road Not Taken*, speaks to the inner moment of choice — one that can influence our lives in ways we don't always expect.

Rather than quoting his words directly, I let their spirit guide the intention behind this piece — an unspoken reflection on listening inward and choosing what feels true.

This creation, like the poem that inspired it, speaks to the power of trusting our own way — even when it means diverging from what's expected.

Threads of Becoming

We are not woven whole from the start.
We become, thread by thread —
through presence, through practice, through possibility.

— Flow-Inspired Reflection

As you sit with fibres in your hands, something quiet begins to stir. The textures, colours, and patterns you choose may seem simple at first — but each holds the potential to speak. Weaving becomes a way of noticing, choosing, and connecting.

The thread you reach for might echo a moment, a relationship, or a turning point. The softness of wool, the roughness of hemp, the brightness of a dyed cord — each one carries its own energy. You may find yourself drawn to contrast: smooth against coarse, muted beside bold. And in the act of placing one thread after another, decisions are made. Paths shift. Patterns form. Just like in life, you may change direction, unpick a section, or add a new element altogether. Weaving becomes a way of reflecting on how your choices — however small — inform something larger.

Across cultures, weaving has long symbolised connection, belonging, and meaning. In myths, it often appears as a metaphor for destiny or creation. Among First Nations people, weaving is deeply rooted in Country, community, and ancestral knowledge. It's a sacred act — one that carries memory, story, and identity. Around the world, threads have linked people to land, to one another, and to something beyond words.

When you weave, you enter that lineage. You add your own voice to the rhythm of a timeless tradition. It doesn't have to look a certain way. There's no one right technique. Some may use large looms, others may finger-weave, or explore digital tools. What matters is how it feels to you. What matters is that you showed up — and listened to what's ready to be expressed.

Some people find that weaving holds not only the present moment, but also glimpses of the future. When you weave with intention, hopes and dreams can begin to take form — woven into something visible and grounded. And when the pattern shifts — because life always does — you can adjust, add a new thread, or simply pause. The future isn't fixed. It's something you create gently, thread by thread.

And though weaving may be solitary, it has always had the power to bring people together. In homes, villages, and sacred spaces, weaving has sparked laughter, conversation, and belonging. Each person contributes their strand. The resulting fabric becomes a reflection of both individuality and unity.

As you continue your own creative journey, you might find that weaving offers more than form. It offers a way of sensing, choosing, and belonging. You're not just making something — you're becoming something. Not through perfection, but through presence.

And so, as your hands meet the loom...
a new story begins to stir.

Reflections in the Weave: Threads of Storytelling

Imagine sitting before an empty loom, the threads waiting for your touch. Each one holds a possibility — a whisper of a story, a glimpse of a memory, or a spark of creativity. There are no rules, no perfect design to follow. Instead, weaving invites you to wander, play, and let your hands lead the way.

Think of the fibres as threads from your life, each one carrying its own texture and hue. Some are smooth and vibrant, alive with joy. Others are rougher, muted, perhaps tangled with challenges. But together, they form something whole — something uniquely yours.

As you prepare to weave, pause for a moment. What threads from your story call to you today? Perhaps it's a colour that feels grounding or a pattern that sparks curiosity. Trust your instincts and let the materials guide you. Weaving is about the act of discovering the patterns waiting to unfold.

With each thread you place, you're not just weaving fabric — you're weaving new ways of seeing. Just as patterns take shape through tension and release, so too can your perspective shift, guiding you toward the life you're crafting.

This is your time to explore, reflect, and create without expectation. Let the rhythm of weaving carry you into a place where stories emerge naturally, thread by thread.

Thread by Thread: Weaving Your Story Into Being

Step 1: Gather Your Materials

Begin your weaving process by choosing materials that resonate with you. Each item you select contributes to the unique story you're about to create:

- **Fibres**: Traditional yarn, wool, embroidery thread, or recycled fabric scraps.
- **Found Objects**: Beads, buttons, leaves, shells, or trinkets with personal meaning.
- **Natural Elements**: Tree branches, dried grasses, or hemp.
- **Optional Additions**: Paint or stain for your branch to add a personal touch.

As you gather materials, reflect on the feelings, memories, or ideas they evoke. These will form the threads of your story. If a memory feels tender or difficult, there's no need to linger in the details — simply notice what golden seam it may hold. What strength, insight, or shift emerged from that experience? Let that become part of what you weave.

Step 2: Create Your Loom
You don't need a traditional loom to get started. Here are a few simple options:

- **Cardboard Loom**: Cut notches along the edges of a sturdy piece of cardboard to hold your threads.
- **Stick Loom**: Use a Y-shaped branch as your frame for a nature-inspired design.
- **Ready-Made Loom**: If you prefer a more conventional approach, find a loom at a craft store.

Need a hand in making and setting up your loom? You'll find lots of beginner-friendly tutorials online — just search for 'DIY loom set-up' or 'simple weaving tutorials.'

Step 3: Set Up Your Warp
- Tie one end of your thread securely to one side of your branch or loom.
- Stretch the thread to the opposite side, leaving space between strands, and tie it securely.
- These vertical threads, called the "warp," create the structure for your weaving. Don't worry about perfect spacing, as imperfections add character.

A Moment to Centre and Ground

Before you begin weaving, take a moment to connect with your inner flow. This practice will help you approach your creation with intention and mindfulness:

1. **Find a Comfortable Position**: Sit comfortably with your feet flat on the floor and your hands resting on your lap. Close your eyes or soften your gaze.
2. **Take Three Deep Breaths**: Inhale deeply through your nose, filling your lungs, and exhale slowly through your mouth, releasing tension. Repeat this step two more times.
3. **Feel the Connection to Your Inner Flow:** With closed eyes, take a moment to notice the rhythm of your breathing and the steadiness of your body. Imagine yourself as part of a larger current of creativity, where ideas and inspiration flow naturally. Let this sense of connection steady you, bringing clarity and focus as you prepare to begin.
4. **Set an Intention**: What do you hope to bring into this weaving practice today? Is it curiosity, peace, or a sense of self-expression? Gently hold this intention in mind, allowing it to guide your hands and heart as you weave.
5. **Return to Your Breath**: Take one more deep breath. When you're ready, open your eyes and bring this centred energy to your weaving.

Step 4: Start Weaving
Now, let the creative process begin!

- **Guide Your Weft**: Use your chosen fibres and a small stick or shuttle to guide the weft thread over and under the warp.
- **Experiment Freely**: Try different textures, colours, and patterns. Incorporate beads, trinkets, or shells to add depth and symbolism.
- **Embrace Imperfections**: Knots, uneven stitches, or unexpected changes can symbolise resilience and add richness to your story.

Step 5: Reflect as You Weave
Weaving is a meditative process of self-discovery.

- **Metaphor for Life**: Each thread represents a decision, experience, or connection.
- **Textures and Colours**: Reflect on what they evoke emotionally or symbolically.
- **Rhythm**: Let the repetitive motion of weaving ground you — bringing clarity and calm.
- As you weave, do any personal stories, emotions, or insights arise? What feels most meaningful or helpful in what surfaces for you? — Try weaving that into your creation.

Step 6: Finish and Display Your Creation
1. Tie off the last threads and trim any loose ends.
2. Step back and admire your work. Reflect on the feelings, memories, or aspirations it represents — and what personal meaning might be woven through it now.

3. Choose a place to display your weaving — wall, window, garden — to affirm what you've woven. Naming it can deepen that sense of meaning.

Step 7: Share Your Creation (Optional)
Want to explore this further? You're invited to share your insights at www.flow-inspired-creations.com.au.

Helpful Hints
Curious to keep weaving, both creatively and personally? You'll find a wide range of resources online — from tutorials and visual guides to community spaces that explore weaving methods. You're also welcome to connect through my website for inspiration or support.

Snapshot: Treasuring Fluidity

In this blended story, we explore how the creative weaving process can reveal hidden potential, empowering someone to exceed even their own expectations. For this narrative, we'll call the main character Alex.

Alex has always approached life with curiosity and creativity. While some aspects of learning didn't come easily, Alex found an outlet in tactile and visual expression, particularly weaving. What began as a simple activity quickly transformed into something more — a way to communicate emotions, ideas, and stories that felt difficult to express through words alone.

As someone who embraced the fluidity of identity and creativity, Alex felt most at home when working intuitively.

Their weaving journey followed the essence of flowcrafting, focusing on the process rather than the end result. They allowed themselves to work freely with fibres, exploring textures, colours, and shapes without attachment to what the final piece would look like. However, as Alex's creations grew, they gradually saw that the results carried a beauty and depth that went far beyond what they had thought possible. The pieces became intricate expressions of their inner world, resonating deeply with both Alex and those around them.

Encouraged by a supportive community, Alex began exhibiting their woven art in galleries, receiving widespread recognition and praise for the originality and beauty of the pieces. The art spoke for itself, and Alex's talent led to multiple awards, including a prestigious arts prize — a testament to the depth and skill they brought to each creation. What made Alex's evolution even more remarkable was the way they continued to grow beyond what others — and perhaps most of all, they themselves — ever expected.

Alex's story celebrates ability, showing how the creative process can unlock hidden strengths and reveal talents that might otherwise remain undiscovered. Through weaving, Alex has found not only a powerful form of self-expression but also a path to thriving and inspiring others by being who they are unapologetically. Their practice stands as an example of the boundless potential within each of us, waiting to be woven into something extraordinary.

Closing Thought: Weaving Together Life's Threads

As we bring this chapter to a close, I hope you've begun to see weaving as more than a craft — it's a way of engaging with the threads of your own life. Each fibre you choose carries meaning: the joys that uplift, the hardships that strengthen, and the transformations that carve your path. Together, these threads form a story that is uniquely yours.

Reflecting on my own experience with weaving, I remember how creating *Two Roads Diverged in a Wood* helped me embrace the beauty of choices and resilience in uncertainty. Just as Robert Frost's poem inspired that piece, weaving itself has a way of inviting us to explore the paths we've taken and the ones yet to come. Alex's snapshot story further reminds us how weaving can celebrate ability, reveal hidden strengths, and transform fragments into something whole and meaningful.

Weaving invites us to gather the fragmented parts of our story, seeing the threads not as separate strands, but as part of an evolving tapestry — one influenced by courage, intention, and flow. Whether you're using yarn, found materials, or weaving with others, this practice creates space for reflection, renewal, and a deeper connection to your inner flow — and to believing in yourself courageously.

Threads to Carry Forward

1. **Weaving is a profound metaphor for life**, illustrating how diverse experiences interweave to create something whole and meaningful.

2. **Each thread represents a part of your story**, adding texture, colour, and richness to your personal tapestry.

3. **Imperfections in your weaving mirror life's ups and downs**, showing how beauty and resilience can emerge from unexpected challenges.

4. **Weaving fosters connection** — to yourself, your narrative, and the deeper flow of creativity and growth.

As you continue your weaving chapter, take time to reflect on each thread you choose. Celebrate the imperfections and honour the strength and beauty they reveal. Let this practice speak to the truth that your story is an ever-evolving tapestry — woven with courage, intention, and the flow of your unique creativity.

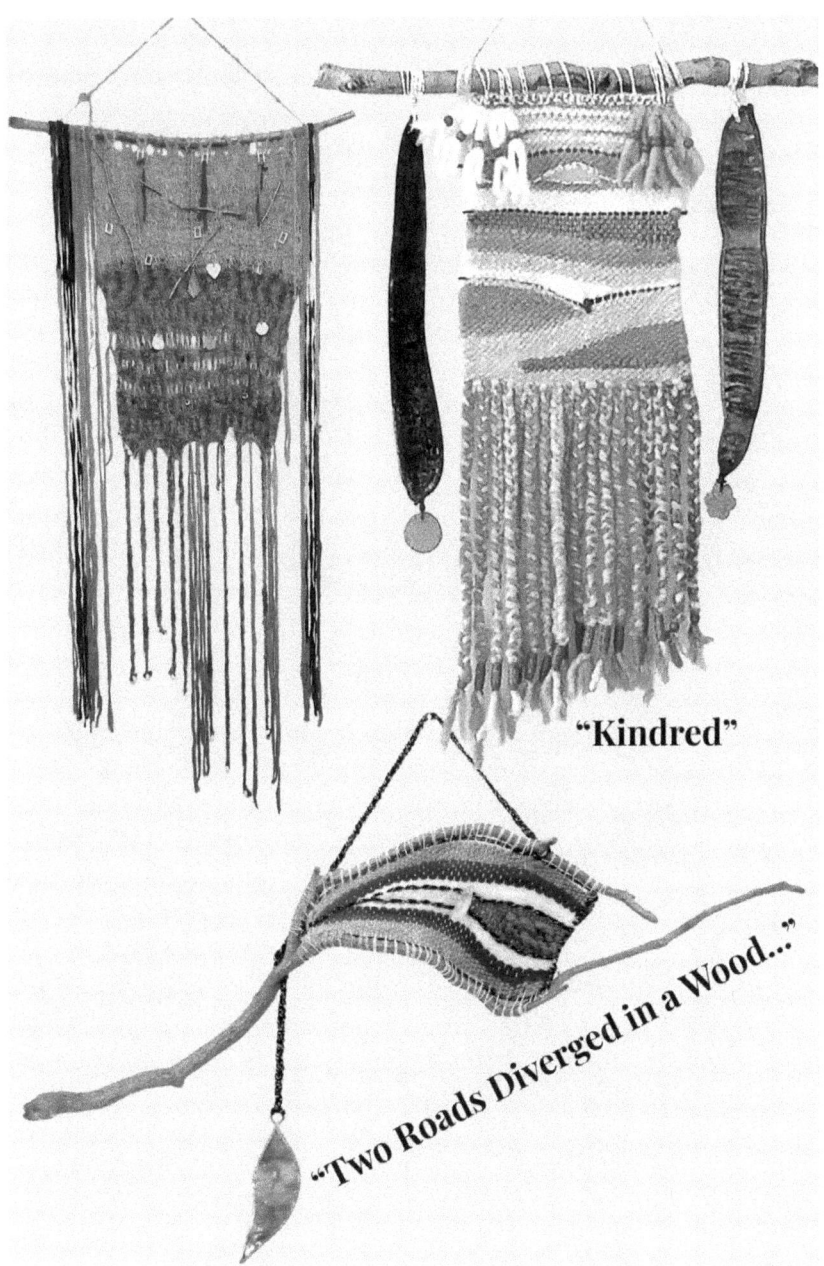

Image 8 **"Weaving Stories into Being"** – Artworks by the author

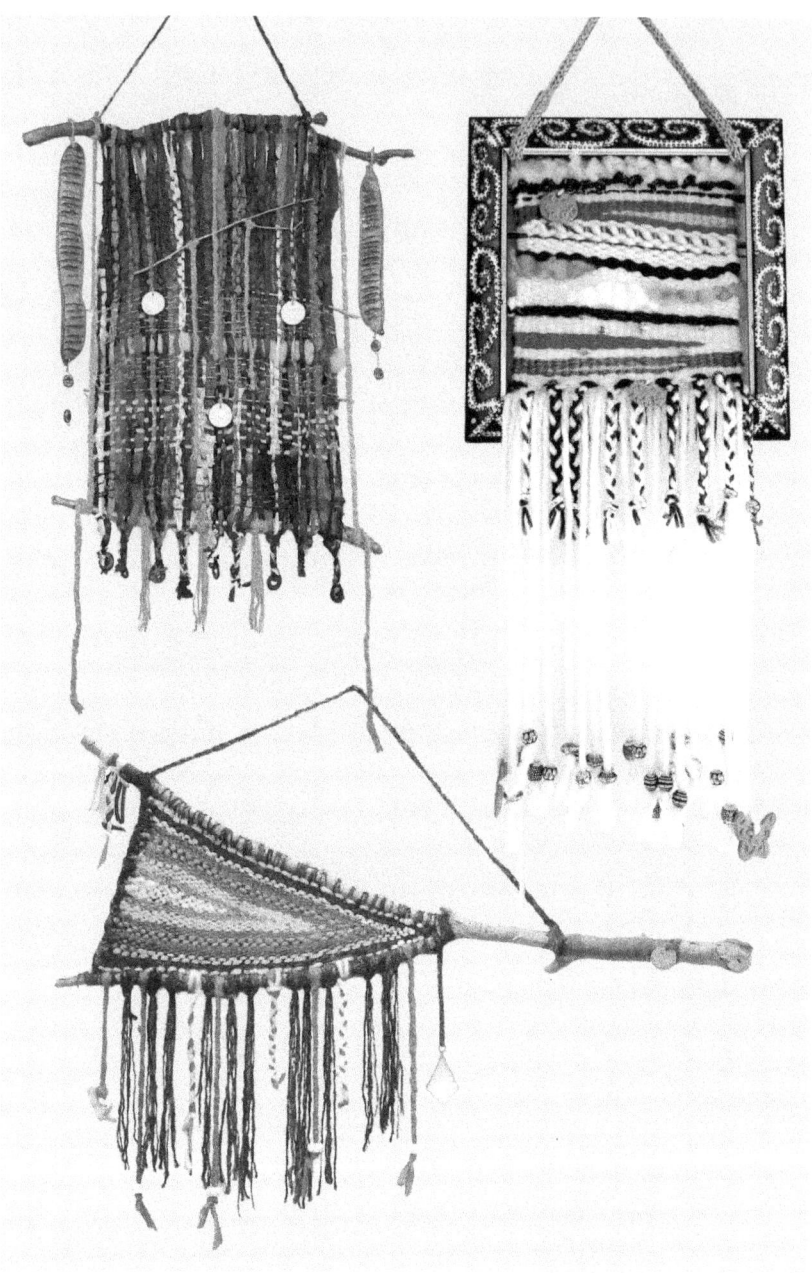

Image 9 **"Weaving Stories into Being 2"**
– Artworks by the author

Drawing Calm From Chaos

*"Inside the tangle, there's always a thread of clarity —
listen closely to what it may reveal."*

– *Flow-Inspired Reflection*

Structured Patterns: A Creative Sanctuary

Life is made up of countless interwoven experiences, emotions, and thoughts — each forming part of a larger, ever-evolving picture. At times, it may feel complex or uncertain. But then, patterns begin to emerge. Just as repeating shapes and lines can bring harmony to a blank page, noticing the rhythms in our experiences can help us navigate life with greater clarity and flow.

In this chapter, we'll explore Flow-Inspired Creations with patterns — a practice that transforms simple shapes into intricate designs. This method allows beauty and clarity to emerge from chaos. Creating structured patterns invites us to slow down, be present, and reconnect with ourselves in grounded, meaningful ways.

By immersing ourselves in the mindful, rhythmic motions of drawing patterns — whether on paper or with digital tools — we step into a flow state where time dissolves. This becomes a space where we can let go of perfection and embrace curiosity. Patterns begin to guide us to uncover insights about what resonates with us, revealing a deeper connection to our preferences, feelings, and inner flow. By flowcrafting patterns, we carve out a sanctuary of creativity — a space where clarity, calm, and self-awareness can emerge in the midst of life's complexities.

Tracing the Lines: How Patterns Carve Clarity

I first encountered pattern-based drawing during a significant period of change in my life. At that time, I found myself moving frequently, never staying in one place for more than a couple of years. I had recently relocated to a new town, and stepped into a therapeutic support role that felt precarious — a role where things were constantly shifting, with little sense of stability. At the same time, a long-term relationship had just ended, leaving me feeling both unsettled and adrift.

Though much was changing around me, my counselling practice remained a place of steadiness — a space where I could offer grounded presence to others, even as I navigated shifts in my own life. Alongside individual sessions, I facilitated regular support groups for caregivers — spaces where participants could bring forward the themes that mattered most to them. One recurring thread was their longing for ways to calm their minds and "tune out" from the ongoing demands they faced.

It was around this time that a colleague introduced the Zentangle[14] method in one of my Carer group sessions. This structured approach to creating patterns, designed to promote relaxation, was warmly received. I, too, felt drawn to it — not just for its techniques, but for the philosophy it embodied.

What captivated me most was not the technique alone, but the philosophy woven through it: there were no mistakes only opportunities to adapt.

If an unexpected mark appeared, it was not an error but a doorway — the design simply evolved around it. That idea found a deep place within me. Later I attended a workshop with a Certified Zentangle Instructor — not to master the method, but to deepen my experience of creativity as a fluid and forgiving process.

Over time, my own way of working with patterns began to evolve — a form of Flow-Inspired Creation that I've come to call flowcrafting. What once felt structured became more intuitive, fluid, and exsspressions of inner flow.

Flow Lines: Patterns as Guides to Insight

During that unsettled chapter of my life, flowcrafting patterns became my lifeline. When words fell short of capturing the whirlwind inside me, the quiet act of drawing repetitive lines and shapes offered me a way to make sense of uncertainty. These relaxing patterns became steady companions on my path to find clarity, calm, and the courage to navigate a tumultuous time.

One of the most transformative aspects of flowcrafting patterns is the way it suspends time itself. Drawing patterns allowed me to step into the unknown and invite unexpected outcomes to emerge. By focusing on basic elements — lines, dots, and curves — the meditative, repetitive motion gave rise to creations that were unplanned yet deeply revealing. It softened my self-doubt and loosened the grip of perfectionism, turning the process into an easeful space of calm and creative freedom.

What I cherished most was its accessibility — a creative space where I could show up just as I was.

Gratitude too wove itself into the practice. Taking a moment to honour the tools in my hands and the unspoken space they opened helped me stay present, finding meaning in each creation, regardless of the outcome. This focus on gratitude brought a groundedness that became a vital part of my wellness spiral.

For some time, I worked with 10x10 cm squares — small, portable paper canvases that at first felt restrictive, but soon revealed themselves as full of possibility. Initially, the limited space seemed to confine me. Over time, though, I realised that within those boundaries, new freedoms could arise. The boundaries of the square became a catalyst, unlocking abilities I hadn't known were there and inspiring a deeper sense of focus and flow.

This small format became a natural companion during my transitions. Tucked easily into a bag or pocket, it was always ready when inspiration stirred. Its compact size allowed me to immerse myself fully in the moment, bringing calm and clarity wherever I happened to be. As my practice evolved, so too did the formats I explored, allowing flowcrafting patterns to grow alongside my becoming.

As I continued to engage with patterned flow, the experience deepened. Letting go of rigid constraints, I found creativity unfolding. Each pattern became a story; each line, a subtle thread weaving its way toward insight and belonging. In reconnecting with inner flow, I found that clarity and inspiration could emerge effortlessly.

To my surprise, one of my flowcrafted pattern designs was selected, sold, and awarded at a local art exhibition — an unexpected outcome from what began as a search for calm and clarity. These small affirmations helped restore a sense of order. Around that time, I enrolled in a Cert IV in design at TAFE (community college), while continuing my private practice. It marked a kind of renewal — a creative outlet that arrived just when I needed it.

That is the subtle power of flowcrafting with patterns — it opens doors you never thought to knock on. What began as a basic, steadying practice became a still source of clarity and creativity — helping me transform uncertainty into a pathway of discovery.

I hope it offers the same for you.

A Few Flow Lines to Spark Your Own

Straight or curved, wonky or neat — each line carries its own rhythm. Let them whisper the possibility that calm begins with one simple mark.

*Some squiggle, some zig, some drift like a breeze.
You never know where a little line might lead.*

Flowcrafting With Patterns: An Introduction and Practice

Flowcrafting with patterns opens a doorway into playful exploration. Curved, diagonal, dashed, dotted, zigzag, horizontal, wavy, parallel, straight, or perpendicular — every line style becomes part of your unfolding rhythm. Vary the thickness and character of your lines as you wish, letting movement and stillness dance together across the page. While other practices may assign names or meanings to specific patterns, here, there are no rules — only your experience.

Trust your heart, let your hands guide — your personal interpretation is what matters most.

For further inspiration, you may like to revisit chapters *"The Place I Went To make Sense"* and *"When Symbols Speak"*, where we explored patterns and symbols drawn from the living artistry of nature.

Movement offers another dimension to explore. Let your patterns meander, ripple, or surge — as subtly or as boldly as they wish to move through you. You might even find delight in playing with negative space, drawing around what isn't there, and watching new forms rise.

Beginning with a moment of gratitude — honouring the tools in your hands — paper, pen, tablet, or stylus, and the invitation to create — can be especially grounding.

If the open space of a blank page feels daunting, offer yourself an easeful beginning: place a small dot in each corner, about half a centimetre from the edge. Connect the dots with a freehand pencil line — curving or straight, whatever feels true in the moment. Let your lines move naturally, without a ruler's constraint. Then, draw a thread or "string" across the page, meandering as it wishes — a wavy, zigzagging, or serpentine path, dividing your canvas into smaller spaces of possibility.

Once your sections are outlined, you can begin to fill them. Let your black ink pen trace patterns into the spaces, one careful line at a time. Colour can come later if you wish — for now, simply follow the quiet rhythm of your hand. Release any grasping for a perfect outcome. Let each line be enough, just as it is.

And when surprises find their way onto your page, welcome them. Shift course if you need to — there are no mistakes here, only new beginnings.

There is no single way to flowcraft with patterns. Rotate your paper, turn it upside down — explore the shifting perspectives. When your piece feels whole, you might deepen it by shading a few areas or adding a wash of colour. And if your heart calls you to, weave your initials into the design — your subtle signature of belonging.

After you've created your design, pause for a moment. Breathe in the wonder of what you've brought to life.

Step-by-Step Exercise

If you feel drawn to begin your own flowcrafted pattern now, the following steps offer a modest guide. Let them support your experience, not constrain it. Skip, adapt, or revisit them as needed — this is your space, and your rhythm leads the way.

Step 1: Centring with Intention
- Find a quiet, comfortable place to begin your flowcrafting with patterns.
- Close your eyes and take a few deep breaths, allowing your body to relax and your mind to settle.
- Set an intention for this practice. Whether it's to explore new patterns, reflect on a recent experience, or simply enjoy the process, let this intention guide your practice.
- Take a moment of gratitude for your tools, surroundings, and time. Let this sense of appreciation infuse your practice.

Step 2: Draw Inspiration from Nature
- If you're unsure where to begin, recall the *"Inner Reflections, Outer Patterns"* exercises in the chapter *"The Place I Went to Make Sense"* and draw ideas from nature. Notice cloud formations, parsley leaves, or wood grain patterns (be playful). Let these organic

forms inspire your own unique patterns without feeling the need to replicate them exactly.

Step 3: Choose Your Tools
- Select tools that suit your style. Fine liners in various thicknesses work well depending on the level of detail you wish to achieve. For detailed, intricate line work, 0.1 or 0.2 archival ink pens are ideal. Digital tools allow for easy adjustments, making space for experimentation, while pencils offer depth and shading options.

Step 4: Start with Basic Patterns
- Begin with basic lines or shapes, allowing your hand to move naturally. Trust your intention to subtly guide each mark you make.

Step 5: Experiment with Details
- If you feel inclined, you can start refining your patterns with a thinner pen or a stylus (if you're drawing on a tablet) or layer elements for complexity. And if it feels right, add colour with gel pens or coloured pencils. Focus on the pleasure of creating and let the patterns evolve naturally.

Step 6: Gratitude and Reflection
- As you finish, take a step back to appreciate your creation. Reflect on how the practice connected you to the present moment or revealed new insights. You might jot down a

few sentences about what you discovered, or simply sit in gratitude for the experience.

If you feel moved to share your creation, I would love to hear from you.

Snapshot: Flowing Into Self-Acceptance

In this blended story, we explore how Flow-Inspired Creation with patterns can foster calm and focus. For this narrative, we'll call the main character Sophie.

From an early age, Sophie noticed her mind worked differently from others around her. Her mind constantly swirled with ideas and questions that set her apart but often left her feeling untethered. Growing up, she struggled to focus on tasks and often felt overwhelmed, as though her mind was racing faster than she could catch up with. Although her creativity shone brightly, she found herself dismissing her talents, focusing instead on the ways she felt she couldn't quite measure up.

After a particularly challenging week at work, Sophie attended a workshop on flowcrafting with patterns. She was sceptical at first — how could drawing basic lines and shapes help manage the chaos she felt inside? But something surprising happened as she sat down with a pen and a small square of paper. Without any particular goal, she began to draw: zigzags, waves, dots — one stroke at a time. Slowly, her breathing steadied, and the usual noise in her mind began to quiet.

The repetitive, mindful motion of creating patterns was soothing. For the first time in a while, Sophie found herself fully present in the moment. There was no pressure to succeed or "get it right." Instead, the process felt freeing. She realised that she didn't need to control her thoughts — she could simply let them flow, just as her pen moved freely across the page.

In the weeks that followed, Sophie made flowcrafting patterns a regular practice. Each morning, she set aside a few minutes to draw before starting her day. These small moments of creativity helped her feel grounded and focused, providing a sense of calm that carried into her daily life. Over time, she began to see herself differently. The same qualities she once viewed as challenges — her quick-thinking mind, her ability to see connections others missed — now felt like gifts. Her patterns, unique and dynamic, reflected the way her mind worked, and she began to take pride in the creativity they represented.

In her practice of flowcrafting patterns, Sophie found the clarity to reimagine her personal narrative. She opened to her individuality and saw herself as someone who had gifts. Her creative practice became a mirror, reflecting her strengths back to her and helping her navigate life's ups and downs with greater ease.

Sophie's journey is an example of the transformative power of flowcrafting patterns. By letting go of expectations and embracing the flow, she discovered a new way to see herself — a perspective anchored in self-acceptance, resilience, and creativity. Today, her patterns are not just a personal practice but a way to share her story, inspiring others to find their own clarity and connection through creativity.

Closing Thought: Clarity Through the Flow of Patterns

In this chapter, we explored how flowcrafting patterns offers a unique pathway to clarity and calm amidst the complexities of life. By engaging in repetitive shapes and lines, this practice can transform into a meditative experience where each stroke becomes a step toward presence, insight, and inner peace.

Whether you choose conventional materials like ink pens and paper or prefer digital tools, this method provides a versatile way to centre yourself and reconnect with the rhythm of the moment. The flow of patterns allows you to find order within chaos, gently reshaping your perspective and embracing a deeper sense of balance.

Threads to Carry Forward

1. **Patterns as Pathways to Clarity**
   Structured patterns offer aesthetic beauty, but more than that, they create a space where complexity can be simplified, helping you make sense of life's many layers.

2. **Unique Expressions in the Moment**
   Each flowcrafted pattern is a one-of-a-kind expression, reflecting where you are in the moment. Your designs and outcomes will be different each time, uniquely yours, and deeply tied to your present state of mind.

3. **Flow as a Gateway to Calm**

    Flowcrafting patterns is an absorbing practice that draws you into the present moment, where time seems to disappear, nurturing calm and clarity, offering both a creative and meditative relief from the demands of daily life.

    As you continue exploring flowcrafting with patterns, you are invited to embrace the idea that there are no rules — just the joy of discovering your personal rhythm and expression. Let each line be a reflection of your inner unfolding, a testament to your ability to find peace and beauty within life's intricate patterns.

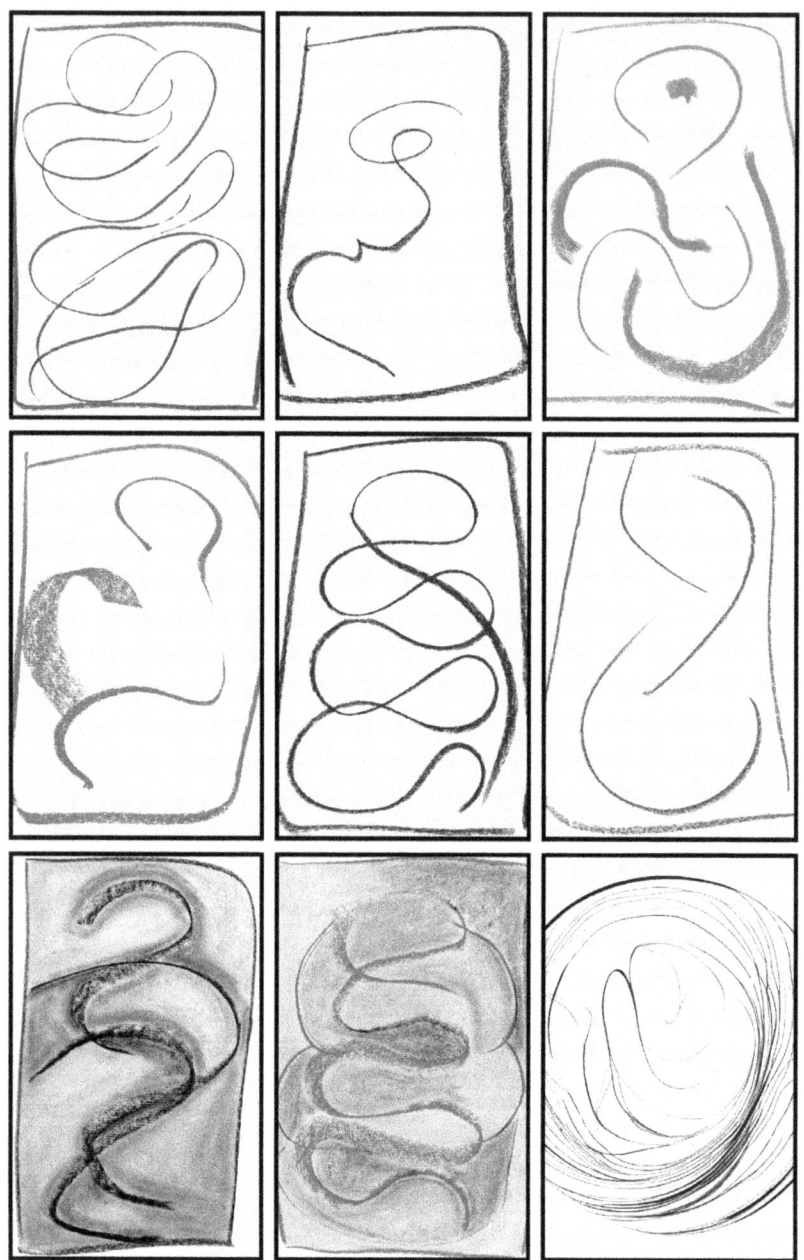

Image 10 **"First Flow: Simple Lines, Endless Possibilities"** – Artworks by the author

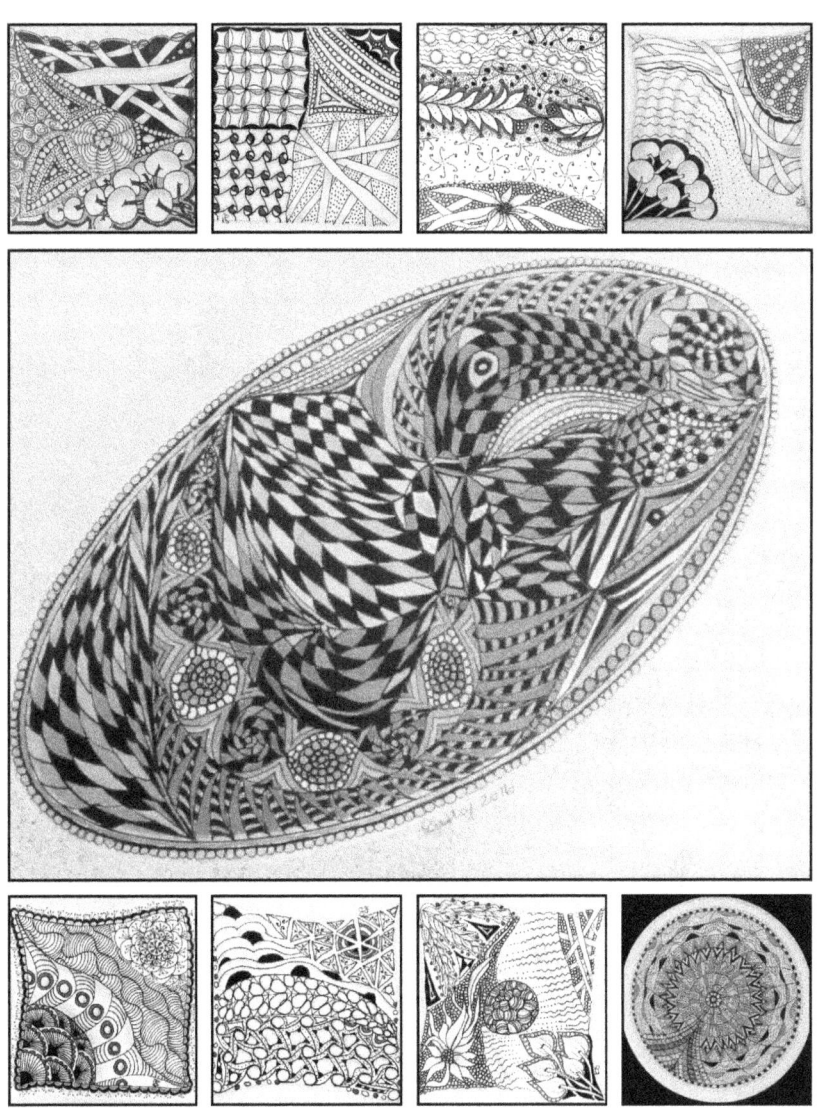

Image 11 **"Line by Line: Creating Calm Through Patterns"** – Artworks by the author

Writing Without Edges

"Sometimes I don't know what I feel until the words find me first."

– *Flow-Inspired Reflection*

Words in Motion

Stories move like rivers — gathering experiences, memories, and emotions along their winding course. They are never static. They flow, weaving themselves into meaning as understanding deepens and new encounters with life unfold.

Writing becomes a way to step into that current, to feel it moving through fingertips and breath.

At times when life felt like a struggle against the flow, free-flow writing became a refuge — a comforting place where words surfaced on their own, finding the paths they had been waiting to travel all along.

Free-flow writing feels like dipping a hand into the stream of an inner voice, letting the currents spill onto the page without judgment or expectation. It is not about crafting perfect sentences, but about discovering the natural rhythm of thought as it unfolds. Word by word, a story takes form — not forced or chased, but allowed to emerge in its own time.

Free-flow writing, as I describe it here, is one form of Flow-Inspired Creation — a kind of flowcrafting with words — following the rhythm of what wants to be expressed.

Unleashing the Flow: Writing Without Boundaries

In moments of uncertainty or hesitation, free-flow writing became an opening — a space where tangled thoughts found their own way forward. It offered me a gateway into discovery, inviting words to land on the page without rules, judgment, or any pressure to perform. Much like other forms of Flow-Inspired Creations, it created room for emotions and insights to surface naturally — often surprising me with what emerged.

Over time, I came to realise how it could shift me into a better feeling place — where thoughts unravel, emotions release, and clarity begins to take shape.

What I discovered through various teachers — and later through my own experience — is that this kind of writing isn't about producing a polished piece. It's about creating a space for self-reflection, healing, and honest inner dialogue. There's no single right way to do it. Some days, your hand might reach for pen and paper; other days, a keyboard may feel more natural. Words might even want to be spoken aloud and captured through a speech-to-text app — freeing them from the mind's internal editing before they slip away.

Written or spoken, the essence is the same — trusting the flow without censorship. It is not grammar, spelling or structure that matters here, but the unspoken courage to release words and let them appear on the page as they are, without judgment.

Free-flow writing is a spontaneous, present-moment practice of seeing where words can lead. It might start with a single word, a phrase, or even a question — and whether it's your pen or your spoken voice (captured through a speech-to-text app), surprising revelations and connections often follow. It's about letting thoughts flow freely, like a stream of consciousness, often leading to unexpected insights and deeper self-understanding.

The Art of Letting Go: My Experience of Flow-crafting with Words

Free-flow writing became a transformative part of my life, though its significance wasn't immediately clear to me. Initially, it served as a bridge, a way to communicate in a new language and reclaim the education I had missed as a child. Navigating the subtle challenge of dyslexia added another layer to my becoming, yet the desire to find connection through words remained strong.

After migrating to Australia, learning English became an unspoken determination. Attending evening classes twice a week built my skills slowly, one lesson at a time. A brilliant, kind English teacher changed everything — someone who celebrated small progress and encouraged every tentative step forward. Her steady belief in me gave me the courage to experiment with language, even when the results felt clumsy at first.

Early Flow-Inspired Creations in writing came in the form of playful poetry and simple prose. Sentences wobbled and wandered, sometimes making little sense, but laughter often followed — and with it, joy. The freedom to create without judgment was enjoyable. It was this joy, not mastery, that paved the way for deeper discovery.

From Gibberish to Flow

I didn't know the rules, so I made my own.
The lines danced and curled — imperfect, playfully, mine.

Even nonsense can carry a rhythm. Later, I would learn that free-flow writing doesn't need grammar — only permission.

No Rules, Just Words

Years later, a creative journal writing workshop with author and teacher Stephanie Dowrick[15], opened another door. Her approach to writing wasn't about perfect sentences or polished stories — it was about honesty, presence, and discovery. In one of her exercises, participants were invited to pick up an object — anything close by — and write about it for five minutes without stopping. "Don't worry about grammar or punctuation," she said. "Just let your thoughts flow." I picked up my pen and began. At first, I wrote about its weight and form, but soon my words veered into unexpected territory. When time was up, I looked at my page and felt a shift. Those five minutes had revealed a knowing I didn't know I had: the ability to express myself without fear or judgment.

From that moment, free-flow writing became a regular part of my life. At home, I'd write in my journal without any agenda. If no ideas came to mind, I'd start with "I don't know what to write..." and repeat it until my thoughts wandered somewhere new. Often, I wouldn't reread what I had written until weeks or months later, and when I did, I was astonished by the clarity and creativity that emerged. Words I couldn't believe were my own seemed to hold unexpected insights and moments of growth.

Over time, this practice became a way of seeing and reimagining my narrative. Above all, it allowed me to shift my focus, change perspective, and uncover new possibilities.

Free-flow writing gave me a way to recognise strengths and possibilities I hadn't fully acknowledged or even recognised before. It became a way to see my resilience, capability, and uniqueness more clearly.

Small Beginnings, Big Discoveries

What began as a simple act of putting pen to paper — writing about an object in front of me — quickly transformed into a thread of insight. My thoughts wandered freely and unpredictably, with no structure or logic, just a steady stream of words spilling onto the page.

When I read back over what I'd written, I discovered unexpected "gems" — small but meaningful reflections that illuminated emotions or experiences I hadn't fully acknowledged. Free-flow writing invited me to remember that creativity doesn't require a clear starting point or a perfect destination. I saw it as a process of uncovering deeper layers of my inner experiences. Through free-flow writing, I was able to see myself from a fresh perspective.

This is the beauty of flowcrafting with words — it invites discovery of our inner landscape. In the process clarity can emerge, new ideas may spark, or simply the joy of letting thoughts dance freely might be enough.

Pages of Possibilities

What if writing was about setting thoughts free to find their own expression? Flow-Inspired free-flow writing invites a release of expectations. Whether scribbling in a notebook, typing on a keyboard, or speaking into a voice recorder, the essence remains the same: letting words flow freely, one after another, without pause for edits or second-guessing. If the blank page feels daunting, remember: this is not about writing a perfect piece, but letting your thoughts land — however they come.

Before beginning with this practice, it helps to create a small, special space, a sanctuary: a favourite notebook, a welcoming page on a tablet, a still moment carved from the day. It helps to create a pocket of uninterrupted time, where your thoughts can wander and your creativity can anchor. With pen, keyboard, or voice, the exploration begins. The stream of consciousness opens — ready to carry whatever wishes to surface.

Opening the Creative Floodgates

Picture a blank page as an open horizon, waiting for the first whisper of story to emerge. Free-flow writing is an invitation to step into this space on a discovery. Words spill out like a river, carrying fragments of your thoughts, emotions, and experiences — some smooth and clear, others raw and tangled. All of it belongs.

It's not about reaching a destination, but about trusting the flow itself to reveal what's waiting beneath the surface. Every sentence becomes a thread woven into the fabric of discovery, adding depth and texture along the way.

What truths will surface when the inner flow is trusted? What unspoken treasures might rise from the depths? This is a space to reflect, create, and to find connection with the rhythm of your own unfolding story.

Let's begin, and see where the flow of words takes us.

Beyond the Blank Page: Approaches to Free-Flow Writing

To ease into free-flow writing, begin with this simple centering exercise to align with your inner flow, cultivate curiosity and openness:

- **Relax with Your Breath**
  Before we begin, take a moment to connect with your inner flow. Sit comfortably and take a deep breath in, then exhale slowly. Repeat until your breathing feels steady and calm.

- **Set Your Intention**
  Reflect on what you'd like to bring into this session. Perhaps it's reclaiming your creative courage, embracing curiosity, or trusting the flow of ideas. With each inhale, invite a sense of possibility; with each exhale, release any pressure to perform.

- **Embrace a Question**
  "What words or thoughts wish to find me today?" Hold this question lightly as you prepare to begin writing.

Various Writing Exercises to Explore

1. Continuous Writing: Let the Words Pour Out
- Set a timer for 5 minutes (gradually increase to 10 or 15 as you grow more comfortable).
- Write continuously without lifting your pen. Refrain from editing. If typing or using a speech-to-txt app, keep going without stopping. If stuck, simply write or say, "I don't know what to write..." until new thoughts surface.
- This exercise is for your eyes only — no need to share unless you choose to.

2. Themed Word Play
- Choose a word or object nearby (e.g., a pen, a window, or an abstract idea like hope or belonging).
- Set a timer and write or speak continuously about the chosen theme, allowing your thoughts to wander freely.
- Don't worry about sticking to the theme — let your mind explore connections and ideas naturally.
- You can also take a book, randomly open a page and take the first word or idea that jumps at you as your theme.

3. Playful Expression
- Be whimsical and light-hearted in your approach. Write or speak playful phrases, abstract musings, or anything that captures the joy of creative flow.

- If stuck, write or say, "I have nothing to say," until your thoughts shift naturally toward new ideas.

Trust that whatever you have written, it belongs. These writings are yours to keep safe — a quiet place for thoughts to land without expectation. You may want to revisit them later. When you do, notice how certain words carry fresh meaning, offer insights, or spark new creative beginnings. This often can be a quiet eye opener.

Snapshot: Writing Toward Clarity

In this blended story, we explore how Flow-Inspired writing can create moments of clarity and strength, empowering someone to reconnect with their inner resilience. For this narrative, we'll call the main character Sarah.

Sarah had always been someone others relied on. Whether managing work deadlines, supporting her close friends through challenges, or simply keeping life's routines on track, she was often the glue that held things together. But over time, the weight of expectations — both from others and herself — began to take its toll. Sarah found herself feeling stretched thin, unsure of where her own needs fit into the equation. It wasn't just the busyness of life that overwhelmed her; it was the growing sense that she had lost sight of herself amidst it all.

One evening, scrolling aimlessly online, Sarah stumbled upon the concept of free-flow writing. She wasn't someone who journaled or wrote regularly, but the idea piqued her curiosity. It wasn't about producing polished writing or even making sense of her thoughts — it was about letting them flow freely, without judgment or expectation. Something about the simplicity of it resonated. Maybe, she thought, it could help her untangle the chaos in her mind.

The next morning, before diving into her usual routines, Sarah decided to try it. She found an old notebook tucked away in a drawer, grabbed a pen, and set a timer for five minutes. The first few lines felt awkward and stilted, her mind resisting the idea of writing anything at all. But she kept the pen moving, even if the words didn't seem to make sense. Slowly, her thoughts began to spill onto the page — frustrations she hadn't voiced, the lingering fatigue she often ignored, and the small moments of joy that had somehow gone unnoticed.

As Sarah wrote, the words started to flow more easily. She found herself reflecting on small quiet moments — the comfort of morning coffee, the way the sunlight danced through her window. By the time the timer buzzed, her page was full — not just with words, but with unexpected clarity. In those five minutes, she had unearthed emotions she hadn't realised she was carrying and glimpsed a part of herself she thought she'd forgotten: her ability to find meaning, even in the messiness of life.

Encouraged by that first session, Sarah started to make free-flow writing a regular habit. Sometimes she wrote about her day; other times, she started with a single word and let her thoughts meander. The more she wrote, the more she noticed how the practice helped her quiet the mental noise and focus on what truly mattered. Her journal became a sanctuary where she could express herself without fear of judgment — a place to explore her thoughts, vent her frustrations, and celebrate her small victories.

Over time, Sarah noticed subtle shifts in her outlook. Flow-Inspired writing had become her refuge, a tool that helped her see challenges as opportunities for growth and connection. Through her writing, she began to reframe her story — not as someone who was always 'holding it all together,' but as someone who was learning, adapting, and thriving in her own unique way.

Her journal filled with raw, honest reflections, but also with insights that sparked hope and inspiration. Through this practice, Sarah realised that while she couldn't control every twist and turn in her life, she could guide the way she responded to them. Writing became her mirror, reflecting the resilience and creativity she hadn't fully recognised in herself. It wasn't just a practice — it was a reminder of her own strength, a space where she could rediscover the beauty of her uniqueness, one word at a time.

Closing Thought: Uncovering Your Story Through Flow-Inspired Writing

Flow-Inspired writing invites us to uncover the layers of our own uniqueness — our perspectives, experiences, and the parts of ourselves that make us who we are. In this chapter, we explored how free-flow writing opens the door to personal insights and creative freedom, offering a space to let our thoughts spill out without boundaries or judgment. By shifting the focus away from polished sentences, to the raw flow of words, we create a path to connect deeply with our emotions and the unique ways we experience the world.

In this chapter we began with experimental, practical exercises to make Flow-Inspired writing accessible to everyone, regardless of your tools or experience. Whether you're using a pen, a tablet, or a speech-to-text app, the key is to embrace the process, allowing words to emerge naturally, uncensored, as a reflection of your inner self.

The personal stories shared here highlight how this practice can be transformative, reshaping how we see ourselves. Flow-Inspired writing encourages us to move beyond old patterns, challenge limiting beliefs, and embark on a process of self-discovery.

Above all, this practice is about letting words lead you to what's yet to be discovered, celebrating the freedom of creative exploration, and finding meaning in the unexpected.

Threads to Carry Forward

1. **Creative Expression Without Judgment:** Free-flow writing is a space for curiosity and exploration, where creativity can unfold naturally and without constraints.

2. **Accessible to Everyone:** Whether you write by hand, use digital tools, or speak your words aloud, this practice is adaptable to your unique preferences and needs.

3. **A Path of Self-Discovery:** Flow-Inspired writing uncovers the stories we tell ourselves, creating opportunities to shift perspectives, challenge limiting beliefs, and reimagine our narratives with clarity and compassion.

As you continue your explorations, know that every word, every line, every moment spent with this practice is a step toward greater connection with yourself. Lean into the process, embrace the flow, and make room for the stories within you to come alive.

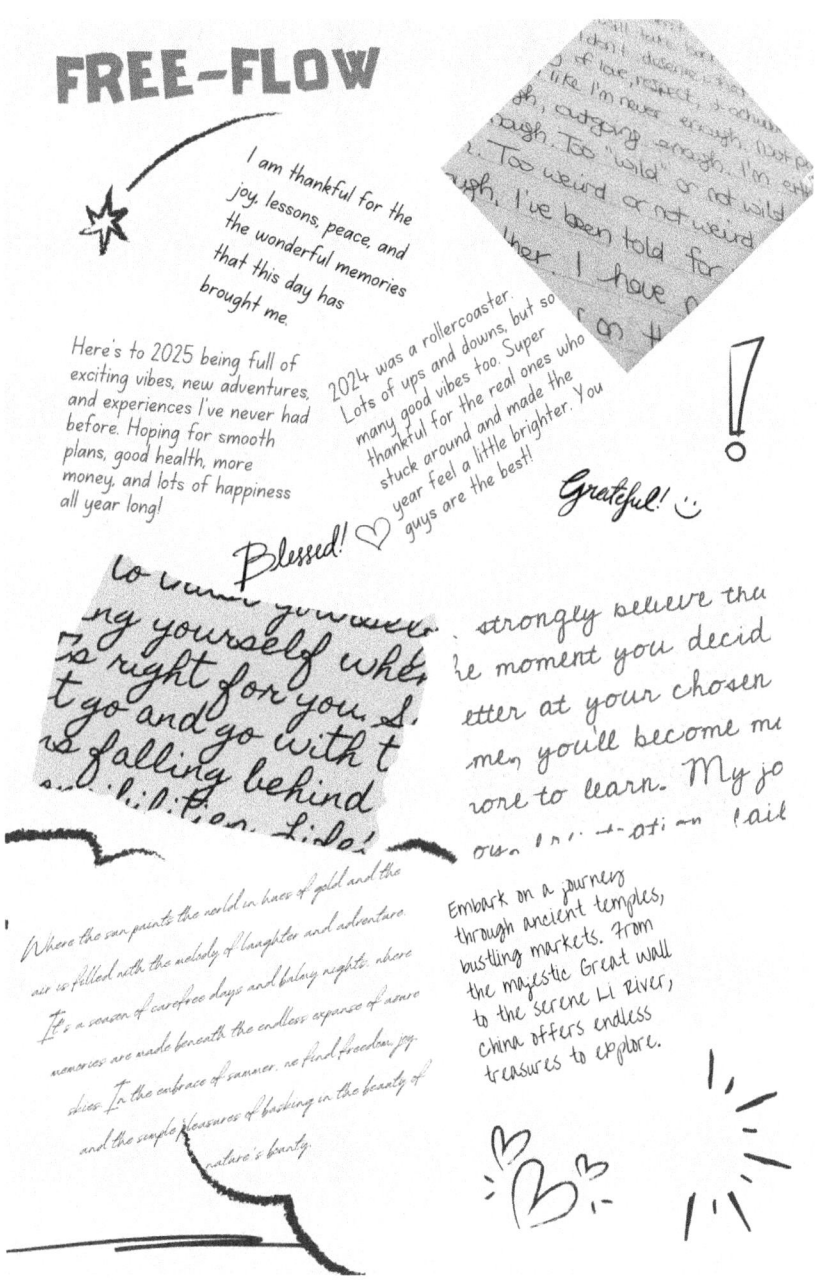

Image 12 **"Uncensored, Unstructured, Unstoppable"**
– A collage composed by the author using digitally adapted Canva Pro elements, reshaped into a flowcrafted visual reflection.

Fleeting Wonders: Nature as Muse

*"Autumn doesn't resist the fall —
it leans gently into the letting go."*

– Flow-Inspired Reflection

Nature: The Ultimate Artist

What breath-taking wonder — standing amidst a forest, the Australian bush, or gazing out at the restless sea — a feeling that stirs a deep knowing within as if nature itself were extending an invitation. Every leaf, every ripple, every shadow cast by the sun is a testament to creation without hesitation, a dance that unfolds without asking permission. Nature does not rush, nor does it wait — it simply becomes, weaving its masterpieces in the wind's embrace, in the soil's unspoken labour, in the rhythm of time itself.

One day, as I wandered through bushland, lost in the stillness, nature's silent genius revealed itself. My gaze fell upon a stone adorned with lichens — tiny, intricate worlds in shades of green and grey, etched as if by an unseen hand. The contours seemed to murmur a truth: that beauty, real beauty, need not serve any purpose other than to be. I remember fumbling for my camera, eager to capture this fleeting marvel, even as I knew that the photograph would never fully hold what I saw or felt. That moment stayed with me — a subtle shift, a recognition of nature as an artist unparalleled, her creations ever-changing, never complete, and yet whole.

In nature, everything is both transient and eternal. A flower unveils its delicate face only for a season, yet its essence endures as seeds scatter and new blooms emerge. The wind sculpts ripples in the sand, only for the tide to erase them, and yet the movement of wind and tide carries on. The fiery hues of a sunset fade as the night stretches its velvet canvas across the sky, but the cycle of light and shadow remains unbroken. Nothing lingers unchanged, yet everything matters. Nature whispers to us in these ephemeral moments, teaching that creativity is not about permanence — it is about presence. It is about the act of becoming.

This, too, is the heart of flowcrafting with nature. When we create in harmony with the natural world, we step into its perfect and timeless cycle, a spacious collaboration with the elements. Each piece we make, each stroke or arrangement, becomes part of a greater story — a story that shifts and reshapes, just as nature does. There is no need to impose a rigid ideal of perfection, because nature, in its endless cycles of becoming and transforming, already embodies it. The joy is in the becoming, the unfolding, the letting go.

As we move within this chapter, let's take a moment to reflect: How has nature touched you? Perhaps it is the way sunlight dances on a stream or the smooth, comforting texture of a stone in your hand. Let these moments speak, guide, and carry the knowing that creativity, like nature, is boundless. It is in the process — in the breath between the beginning and the end — that meaning unfolds. Let nature walk beside us, muse, companion, and artist, trusting in the beauty of what is to emerge.

Flow and the Natural World

At the heart of Flow-Inspired Creations is the state of flow — a sense of complete immersion where time seems to dissolve, and we become fully present in the act of creating. Nature, with its effortless cycles and constant transformations, naturally invites us into this state. Whether we are noticing the curve of a branch, arranging stones into a momentary pattern, or simply observing the interplay of light and shadow, we are drawn into the flow of the moment. This chapter explores how connecting with the natural world can open the door to flow, allowing us to embrace creativity, presence, and the joy of being.

What is Flowcrafting with Nature?

Flowcrafting with nature invites us to use its textures, rhythms, and forms as both canvas and muse. It's a practice that encourages us to dip into our shared toolbox, drawing from nature's infinite resources to spark our creativity in the moment. Together, we engage with what is around us — leaves, water, stones, light, shadows — and welcome these elements to guide our expression.

Flowcrafting with nature honours both the transitory and the eternal. It's about creating in partnership with nature, recognising its timeless cycles and offering respect to its ever-changing forms. A spiral of stones, a pattern traced in the sand, or an arrangement of twigs becomes an expression of connection — a gesture of reciprocity with nature's dynamic flow. These creations may be temporary in form, but they reflect an enduring truth: our place within the eternal cycles of the natural world.

At its heart, this practice is both meditative and spontaneous. There's no need for a fixed plan. Instead, stepping into nature with openness and curiosity allows what we encounter to guide the direction of our Flow-Inspired Creations. As we arrange, transform, and interact with natural elements, we align with the same creative energy that nature embodies — one that is forever shifting, growing, and evolving.

The elegance of flowcrafting with nature lies in its simplicity. No elaborate tools or special skills are required; instead, we work with what's already present. Whether it's tracing the path of a stream, arranging fallen leaves into a mosaic, or simply observing a puddle after the rain, the playful designs disclose themselves to us in profound ways as we engage with the raw materials of the earth. In these moments, our creative acts become deeply personal reflections, while simultaneously connecting us to the larger pulse of life.

This practice is a powerful addition to our creative toolbox. It invites us to see that creativity isn't confined to permanence or possession. It's a way of experiencing and embracing the process, just as nature does. By co-creating with the ever-changing elements of the natural world, we are also learning to embrace the ever-changing phases of ourselves.

Nature as Path to Belonging

For those of us who have ever felt out of place — disconnected from ourselves, our surroundings, or even our own stories — flowcrafting with nature can become a powerful bridge. For me, this connection was deeply personal. There was a time when I struggled to feel a sense of belonging — to a place, a family, or a culture. But, through the unspoken companionship of nature, my reality began to shift. Observing the rhythms of the natural world, I felt a spark — a kindling of kinship that transcended human boundaries and spoke to my essence.

Donna Haraway's[6] reflection that "to be kind is to be kin" deeply resonates with this thread of thought. Her follow-up — "but kin is not kind" — offers a provocative twist, challenging the assumption that kinship automatically guarantees kindness — offering the perspective that while it often does, it does not necessarily. In nature, I began to see kinship not as a truth confined to traditional ideas of family, but as a shared belonging with all "earthlings". This realisation brought me to see that belonging isn't about finding a fixed place — it's about experiencing connection: within ourselves, with others, and with the living world around us. And I would say that true belonging begins within — when we feel at home and at ease in ourselves, we can more fully recognise our connection to both people and the greater web of life. My hope is that this perspective will be just as meaningful to you on your path.

Engaging with nature through Flow-Inspired Creations offers a way to rediscover that connection. It provides the permission to step outside the constraints of societal expectations and external validation, anchoring our sense of self in a reality that's vast and enduring. Through observing, creating, and simply being present, we start noticing the beauty not just in the world around us, but also within ourselves.

I've devoted this chapter to exploring nature as muse because, for many of us, that sense of belonging is elusive — an unspoken longing that sways our experiences and perspectives. For me, nature has been more than an inspiration; it has been a teacher, a companion, and a pathway back to myself. My hope is that by sharing these musings in detail, readers who resonate with this longing might find their own spark of connection and belonging in these reflections.

Flowcrafting with nature holds the potential for healing and growth. It invites us to reframe our narratives — not through what we lack, but through what we bring: our strengths, our uniqueness, and the threads of belonging we weave through our experiences. Flow-Inspired Creations in and with nature reveal that adaptability, resilience, and transformation are not just lessons from nature; they are also our birthright.

In the sections that follow, we'll explore diverse approaches to engaging with nature's patterns, unveiling how the interplay of permanence and impermanence, wonder, and interconnectedness becomes a guide toward a deeper understanding of ourselves and our sense of belonging. Flowcrafting with nature invites us to discover belonging in its many forms — as something that has always been within us, waiting to be kindled like a spark in the wind, authentically ours.

My Early Influence: '*Grossvati*'[16] and the Magic of Nature

When I think about my connection to flowcrafting with nature, it's impossible not to begin with my grandfather, *Grossvati*. A quiet man with a deep connection to the natural world, he seemed to carry nature's pulse within him. Though life threw many challenges his way — most notably the fire that claimed their farm (there were no insurance claims in those days), forcing my grandparents to start over in Bern with their ten children — his love for the land never wavered. He transitioned from farmer to carpenter, crafting coffins for an undertaker, yet his soul remained tethered to the outdoors.

Sundays with *Grossvati* were nothing short of magical. When I was 4 or 5 years old, he would take my younger cousin Leila[17] and me on walks through the nearby forest or to the *Bärengraben*[18] in Bern. Always prepared, his pockets held *Kandis-zucker* (raw sugar rock candy) for us and hazelnuts for the squirrels. His knack for summoning squirrels was mesmerising. A rhythmic 'tap-tap' of two hazelnuts was all it took for them to approach, trusting him completely. Leila and I, despite countless attempts, never quite mastered his skill. Standing as still as statues, we watched in awe as he connected with nature in a way that seemed almost otherworldly.

These walks weren't just about feeding squirrels or marvelling at the bears in the pit; they were about the subtle lessons *Grossvati* shared. He showed us how to notice the small details — a bird's song, the patterns of moss on a tree — and wove stories of animals and nature that filled our imaginations. Looking back, I realise he was planting seeds of mindfulness and wonder, lessons I carry with me even now.

A Bond Beyond Time: Lessons That Lasted

When I was 13, living in the children's home, news came that *Grossvati* had passed away in his sleep. Although years had passed since I'd last seen him, his influence lingered. I often thought of him during moments when I felt lost or uncertain.

One particular memory stands out. During my 'defiant' years, after school one day, a group of us girls from the home teamed up to steal from a corner shop — an act we had done before. I joined them in a reckless attempt to fit in. Though hesitant each time, I went along once more, desperate not to be left out. That evening, sitting alone on a swing, I felt a wave of unease. I thought of *Grossvati*, picturing him watching from above, his kind but steady gaze filled with disappointment. It wasn't scolding or guilt I felt, but a still nudge — a reminder of the values he had quietly instilled in me. I promised him in that moment that I would never steal again. And I didn't.

That swing had held more than one turning point in my life. It was there again that evening, when a quiet memory of Grossvati stirred something in me once more.

These promises became more than resolutions; they were turning points. They saved me from choices that led some of the other girls into significant trouble, and they became touchstones — ways to reconnect with the guidance he'd given me, even long after he was gone.

A Full Circle: Rediscovering Nature's Secret

Decades later, my relationship with nature and creativity came full circle. In 2018, I met artist Ali Haigh[19], whose philosophy of ephemeral art resonated deeply. Her practice of "one-a-day" — noticing and appreciating brief moments of natural wonders — felt like a call back to those early lessons with *Grossvati*. It wasn't just about creating; it was about being present, about seeing the extraordinary in the everyday.

Inspired, I began photographing my own discoveries during morning walks on the beach with my dog. The interplay of sunlight, waves, and sand offered endless surprises. A tree stump washed ashore after a storm revealed the silhouette of a meerkat. Another stump cast a shadow that resembled a sleeping dragon. These moments felt like quiet collaborations with nature, as though they were offering glimpses of its artistry to anyone willing to observe.

Even the smallest details — lichens on a rock, tangled roots, or shadows cast by branches — became sources of inspiration. What others might overlook, I saw as ephemeral masterpieces, each offering a glimpse of both the temporary and the enduring presence life holds. Each discovery reinforced a truth that nature and Flow-Inspired Creations share: the process is the art, and the act of noticing is its own reward.

Moments and Continuums: What Nature Quietly Reveals

One of the most profound moments of insight came during a simple conversation. As my gaze drifted from the people in front of me to a nearby wall, I noticed their shadows, impermanent and ever-changing with the movement of the sun. In that moment, the shadows became a metaphor for the delicate interplay of transience and continuity at the heart of flowcrafting in and with nature. While some moments may seem to pass quickly, they are part of a larger cycle where nothing is truly lost — only transformed. This awareness deepened my appreciation for the present, encouraging me to savour each moment while trusting the eternal pattern of change.

That realisation became a cornerstone of how I experience flowcrafting with and in nature. Shadows, like the ephemeral art we create from natural elements, exist only for a moment — yet they embody a timeless truth: everything changes, and everything continues. Shadows rely on the tangible for their existence, yet they remain intangible themselves — a quiet expression of life's ongoing movements. It's within these brief instances that beauty reveals itself most vividly, inviting us to savour the present and find meaning in both the momentary and the enduring.

Capturing these shadows in photographs became one way I began embracing impermanence. Each image felt like a meditation — a study of the delicate balance between light and dark, presence and absence. But over time, I came to realise that flowcrafting with and in nature isn't solely about capturing or creating; it's about listening, noticing, and understanding life itself. It's about seeing the wonder in what fades, in allowing each moment to transform us, and in discovering that even the smallest things can hold extraordinary significance. This practice is a reframe, an invitation to view the world with fresh eyes and find the remarkable within the everyday.

The full realisation of how ephemeral nature and life is, struck me so deeply that I titled my autoethnography *Re-thinking Ephemera: A Look in the Mirror.* Looking in the mirror, meant looking at myself (self-reflection). Even then, though I hadn't yet discovered the term "Flow-Inspired Creations," the seeds of the concept were already present in my thinking. I was captivated by the interconnectedness of life, the way everything — seen and unseen, what's vanishing and enduring — is part of a larger, symbiotic dance and flow.

Studio Olafur Eliasson

One of my greatest inspirations during this time was Icelandic-Danish artist Olafur Eliasson[20] and his exhibition *Symbiotic Seeing.* Renowned for his immersive installations blending light, water, and air, Eliasson's work invites reflection on our interconnectedness with the living world.

Symbiotic Seeing explores how organisms and systems coexist, nurture, and transform one another — a vision that resonates deeply with me and Flow-Inspired Creations in nature. Here too, creativity becomes a shared dance with the environment, shaping and being shaped in return.

It was during the writing of my autoethnography that Eliasson's work first crossed my path — a serendipitous moment sparked by my supervisor's casual mention of his exhibition in Zurich, Switzerland. Unable to attend in person, a dear friend visited on my behalf and later sent me the exhibition catalogue — just days before the gallery closed due to the unfolding pandemic.

This small chain of events — a conversation, a gesture of generosity, an unexpected closure — mirrored the very interconnectedness Eliasson celebrates: how inspiration moves through unseen threads of connection.

During that time, I wrote reflections exploring how life itself is a symbiotic dance — a continual exchange between breath, growth, decay, and renewal. Even before I had the words "Flow-Inspired Creations," the seeds of flowcrafting were already taking root within me — celebrating the interplay between impermanence and continuity. It was the noticing, gathering, and creating that led me to the insight that we belong to life's greater rhythms.

Eliasson prompts us to step outside, to notice the brief wonders around us, and to honour the connections that weave us all together — a living, breathing symphony of life, creativity, and belonging.

Wabi-Sabi[21]: Life's Imperfect Perfection

Earlier, we explored the art of Kintsugi — a philosophy of healing, where brokenness becomes a feature of beauty and resilience. Similarly, Wabi-Sabi is a way of seeing: an invitation to find beauty in imperfection, the unfinished, the rustic and the flawed. It embraces the idea that nothing is perfect or permanent.

Flow-Inspired Creations echo this spirit by inviting us to loosen fixed expectations and find wonder in what is rustic, imperfect.

Fleeting Wonders: Nature as Muse

My first encounter with Wabi-Sabi came through the practice of ephemeral art. While both Kintsugi and Wabi-Sabi honour life's impermanence, Wabi-Sabi draws us closer to the ordinary moments — growth, decay, renewal — and invites us to see them as part of life's essence.

This perspective grew even more meaningful during the early days of the pandemic — a time when certainty dissolved and presence had its own kind of attraction. Wabi-Sabi offered a way to meet change without resistance — to find meaning even when familiar forms were falling away.

There is quiet magnificence in what we often overlook.
A patch of lichens on a rock.
The twisted resilience of weed roots.
The persistence of wildflowers in cracked pavement.
When we pause and truly see, we uncover intricate worlds of life — reminders of our deep belonging to the living world around us.

Flowcrafting invites us to feel our way into presence — to attune to what often goes unseen, and let it move us, so that each fleeting encounter shifts how we experience ourselves and our place in the wider web of life.

Photographing overlooked moments — a cluster of gnarled roots, a weathered leaf, a shadow stretching across stone — revealed to me how much artistry life carries when we allow it to be as it is.

Through the lens of Wabi-Sabi and Flow-Inspired Creations, I came to understand that creativity is not about constructing perfection — it is about witnessing, feeling, and allowing each passing moment to reveal its quiet magic.

This practice deepened my connection to myself and the world. It became more than a creative outlet — it became a way of living. A way of meeting life with openness, curiosity, and a willingness to find wonder in what unfolds, just as it is — where creativity flourishes not in polished perfection, but in the ephemeral, the unexpected, and the living threads of life's shifting patterns. Belonging, too, does not come through striving — it is revealed in the simple act of becoming.

The Beauty of Not Quite

Nothing is perfect — that's part of the grace,
A crack in the surface, a line out of place.
A thread left hanging, a mark left unseen —
These are the spaces where beauty resides.
Nothing is lasting — it shifts and it sways,
Fading like light at the end of the day.
What once felt certain will soften and change,
Becoming a form with room to renew.
Nothing is finished — not really, not yet.
The shape still forming, the ink still wet.
And maybe that's how we're meant to unfold:
Not fully written. Not tightly rolled.
— Flow-Inspired Reflection

Where Do These Little Shapes Come From?

They're not quite wildflowers... but maybe they once were. Someone, somewhere, noticed the curve of a branch, the flick of a petal — and let their pen follow.

A little embellishment, a gentle echo of the natural world. What might you notice, if you looked again?

Too tidy for the forest, too wobbly for the garden —
just right for a moment of playful noticing.

Rewriting the Story of Belonging (to Yourself)

In nature, time unfolds differently — fluidly, cyclically, and without the rigid structures we often impose in everyday life. The seasons shift, plants grow, tides ebb and flow, all following their own rhythm. This natural pacing whispered to me a deeply felt truth: it's okay to move through life at one's own tempo, to embrace our unique patterns, even if they don't align with society's expectations.

Observing nature's effortless diversity revealed another lesson: everything — no matter how small, seemingly flawed, or out of place — has its role, its purpose, and its value. A patch of moss on a rock, the curves of a gnarled branch, the persistence of wildflowers growing through cracks in the pavement — all are embraced by nature exactly as they are. There is no demand to fit in, no reliance to be anyone other than oneself. This permission opened a doorway, to reconsider my own self-perception. I hope it will do the same for you.

Flowcrafting with and in nature gave me the time and space to reflect on my personal narrative. It became a way to 'rewrite' my story — a shift from seeing myself as someone who didn't belong to recognising that my differences were not deficits, but contributions and they belonged exactly as they are. Just as every element of nature plays its part, I began to see my own place in the world as uniquely meaningful.

Creating with nature allowed me to turn around old patterns of self-doubt into self-acceptance. The process of creating in sync with nature — whether arranging leaves, observing shadows, or simply pausing to become aware of the intricate details around me — made me realise that beauty lies in authenticity. It showed me that I didn't need to mould myself to fit the expectations of others; instead, I could thrive by celebrating who I already was.

In your discovery of Flow-Inspired Creations with and in nature, let them become a mirror for your own unfolding path — a way to reframe how you see yourself, through the lens of your unique strengths. My wish is that you may come to own your radiance, your unique rhythm, and the power of your own becoming.

Inspiration from Andy Goldsworthy[22]: Dancing with the Ephemeral

Imagine if impermanence weren't a reality to fear, but a call — an opportunity to live more fully, to move with change rather than resist it. While our Western culture often clings to the idea of permanence — preserving moments, relationships, possessions — nature reveals another way: a playful cycle of creation, transformation, and renewal.

This spirit is beautifully embodied in the work of Andy Goldsworthy, one of the most celebrated ephemeral artists. Using materials like leaves, stones, ice, and twigs, Goldsworthy creates works that exist only briefly before they melt, scatter, or are carried away by wind or water. His art doesn't strive to outlast time; it collaborates with it — accepting change as part of the dance, finding value not in what endures, but in what emerges and dissolves.

Goldsworthy often speaks of how, in his work, elements flow together so seamlessly that it's impossible to tell where one ends and another begins. In this way, his art becomes a living metaphor for life itself — an intricate web where each moment contributes to a greater, evolving whole.

When I reflect on his approach, I see echoes of my own experience: how, just like his creations arise from their surroundings, my life too has been influenced by the landscapes, people, and silent encounters I've gathered along the way. Goldsworthy's work reminds me that wonder is born in presence — in showing up fully for what is here now.

Meaning isn't measured by what lasts, but by what is lived.

As I create with nature, I find myself drawn to what's around me — leaves, stones, shifting shadows — without worrying about whether it will endure. In embracing this ephemeral flow, I've discovered not just the joy of creating, but a deeper sense of ease and acceptance for life's ever-changing patterns.

(If you feel curious to explore more of Goldsworthy's work, his official website offers a beautiful glimpse into the art of living and creating with nature's impermanence.)

Brief Wonders: Co-Creating With Nature

The exercises that follow are about connection — to nature, to the moment, and to yourself. Engaging with nature's passing characteristics opens our eyes to the truth that while change is constant in the observable world, there is also a steady presence beneath it all — a thread that grounds us in the unchanging amidst life's ebb and flow.

Let's carry these ideas of embracing nature's ebb and flow into our creative expressions, discovering how ephemeral art can help us enter a state of flow. By centring ourselves and being fully present with nature, we open a doorway to creativity that is grounded in the here and now — where each moment offers an opportunity to connect, create, and simply be.

Exercise 1: Centring — Embracing Presence in Nature

Before starting with our Flow-Inspired Creations exercises, let's take a moment to align and centre ourselves. Centring creates space for creativity to flow freely, allowing us to connect deeply with nature and ourselves. This is not primarily about doing; it's about being — being present, open, and curious.

Step 1: Find Your Nature Space
- Choose a natural environment that resonates with you. It could be a beach, forest, park, backyard, or even a corner of your home filled with plants or herbs. Urban settings can work too — perhaps a balcony garden or a spot near an open window where you can feel the breeze.
- Take a moment to settle in this space. Whether sitting or standing, let yourself feel connected to the environment, welcoming its calm and vitality.

Step 2: Connect Through Your Breath

- Close your eyes or soften your gaze. Take a deep breath in, allowing calm to fill your body. Exhale slowly, releasing distractions and tensions. Repeat this for a few moments, letting each breath ground you more deeply in the present.

Step 3: Set Your Intention

- Quietly set an intention for your time in nature. It could be as simple as, "I'm here to notice" or "I'm open to connection." This intention doesn't need to be perfect — just a truth that aligns with your present moment.

Step 4: Awaken Your Senses

- Open your eyes slowly and begin to observe. What do you see? Observe the shapes, colours, and movement around you. Listen to the sounds — birds singing, leaves rustling, or water flowing. Feel the textures of bark, earth, or leaves beneath your fingertips. Inhale the scents of the air, soil, or flowers nearby. Become immersed in this sensory experience, letting curiosity guide you.

Exercise 1: Noticing and Being Present in Nature

Start by allowing the natural world to unfold around you. Become aware of the intricate details — the veins on a leaf, the pattern of light filtering through branches, or the glimmer of dew on grass. Let yourself look as if you are seeing these things for the very first time.

If you feel inspired, capture what you observe. You might photograph a moment, trace the outline of a shadow, write a brief description, or poem, or even speak your thoughts into a recording app on your phone. The method doesn't matter as much as the act of noticing, being fully present and receptive.

This practice is about curiosity — embracing the extraordinary in the ordinary. Invite nature to surprise you with its subtle wonders.

Exercise 2: Creating Ephemeral Art with Nature

Let's co-create with nature by crafting an ephemeral artwork. This exercise invites you to use natural materials found around you — stones, leaves, twigs, shells, or even shadows and light — to create a temporary design.

Step 1: Gather Your Materials

Look for elements that catch your eye. Perhaps it's a uniquely shaped rock or a vibrant leaf. Collect what feels meaningful, keeping in mind that this is a momentary creation that will return to nature.

Step 2: Arrange with Intention

Using your materials, arrange them into a design or form. It could be a simple spiral of stones, a playful scattering of leaves, or a delicate balance of twigs and shells. Don't worry about perfection or symmetry — let the arrangement evolve naturally, guided by intuition.

Step 3: Reflect and Capture
Once your creation feels complete, pause to reflect. What does it mean to you? What feelings or thoughts arise as you take it in? If you'd like, write — or speak — your reflections in a journal or voice note to keep. It can be meaningful to revisit them later, especially as your perspective evolves.

Here are some guiding questions to explore:

- What do these brief moments of creation reveal to me?
- How did the process of noticing, gathering, and arranging shift my inner knowing?

As you carry this experience forward, let it inspire you to embrace the rhythm of change. And recognise the subtle belonging that already exists — within yourself, in nature, and in the essence that connects us all.

Vanishing glimpses of nature's pulse can show that change and stillness coexist. As you carry this experience forward, may it deepen your trust in your own flourishing — steady, subtle, and connected to a greater knowing.

I invite you to share your experiences — whether in your personal journal, with a trusted friend, or on my website.

Snapshot: Flowcrafting in Collaboration with Nature

In this blended story, we explore how Flow-Inspired Creations — in collaboration with nature — can bring moments of calm and grounding, opening space to embrace life's ephemeral cycles. For this narrative, we'll call the main character Jess.

Jess, a freelance designer, often felt like her mind was moving faster than the world around her. She thrived on creativity, but the demands of work and social life left her overstimulated, scattered, and unsure how to slow down. Traditional mindfulness practices never quite worked for her — they felt too rigid, too still.

When a friend suggested she try a simple nature-based creative practice, Jess was sceptical. But something in her was curious.

One afternoon, she found herself in a clearing by a creek, surrounded by trees and the soft rustle of wind. With no plan, she began gathering what was around her — a curled leaf, a smooth stone, a fallen flower. As she placed them into a spiral on the earth, something shifted. The act of arranging these fragile, found elements — not to last, not to be perfect — brought an ease she hadn't known she was missing.

Later, when the wind scattered her creation, Jess didn't feel loss. She felt relief. Something in her let go. She'd created something beautiful without control — and that beauty had met her, then moved on.

Over time, Jess made ephemeral Flow-Inspired Creations a regular practice. She found different spots in nature and used what she found to create brief, beautiful patterns that only lasted a few minutes.

Her friend soon noticed a shift in Jess's outlook. She seemed more settled, less distracted, and even brought a new sense of ease to her design work. Flowcrafting with nature had offered Jess a simple yet profound way to slow down, find balance, and embrace the value in both what passes and what remains — the brief radiance of her creation and the steady constancy of the earth beneath it. Through this practice, Jess discovered that while beauty may not be lasting, it arises from an essence that remains constant — a subtle reflection of life's interconnectedness. This peaceful acceptance began to ripple into other areas of her life, allowing a sense of clarity and belonging to grow slowly from within.

Closing Thought: Nature's Inspiration – Creating Art from the World Around Us

In this chapter, we explored the profound ways nature connects us to creativity and flow. Nature, as the ultimate artist, teaches us acceptance, transformation, and presence in both impermanence and continuity. By observing the cycles and diversity in nature, we see that everything — no matter how small or unconventional — has value and a role to play in the ever-evolving story of life.

Flowcrafting with and in nature encourages us to pause, become aware, and connect deeply with the world around us. Through practices like mindful observation and creating temporary art from natural materials, we're invited to let our senses guide us, immersing fully in the moment. These ephemeral creations invite us to see that beauty often emerges through the interplay of change and constancy — and that the act of flowcrafting with nature can hold meaning far beyond the final result.

This chapter also drew inspiration from Andy Goldsworthy's ephemeral art, which beautifully embodies its core themes. The philosophy of interconnectedness mirrors our own becoming: just as materials, process, and place are inseparable, so too are we deeply connected — to one another, and to the world around us.

Threads to Carry Forward

1. **The Power of Presence**: Engaging with nature centres us in the present, opening the door for creativity to flow.

2. **Ephemeral Art as a Mirror of Life:** Temporary art invites us to welcome the passing nature of things, while recognising the quiet continuity within change.

3. **Interconnectedness**: Nature's web of connections inspires us to recognise our unique qualities — our abilities, perspectives, and experiences — and how they add to the richness of the whole.

4. **Personal Growth through Flow-Inspired Creations**: By engaging with nature and discovering its lessons, we can reframe our personal narratives, fostering self-discovery, belonging, and purpose.

As you move forward with Flow-Inspired Creations, let nature be both guide and companion. Just as the seasons shift effortlessly, we too can embrace each moment with curiosity, creativity, and rest in the knowing that we are always part of something greater, always evolving, always belonging.

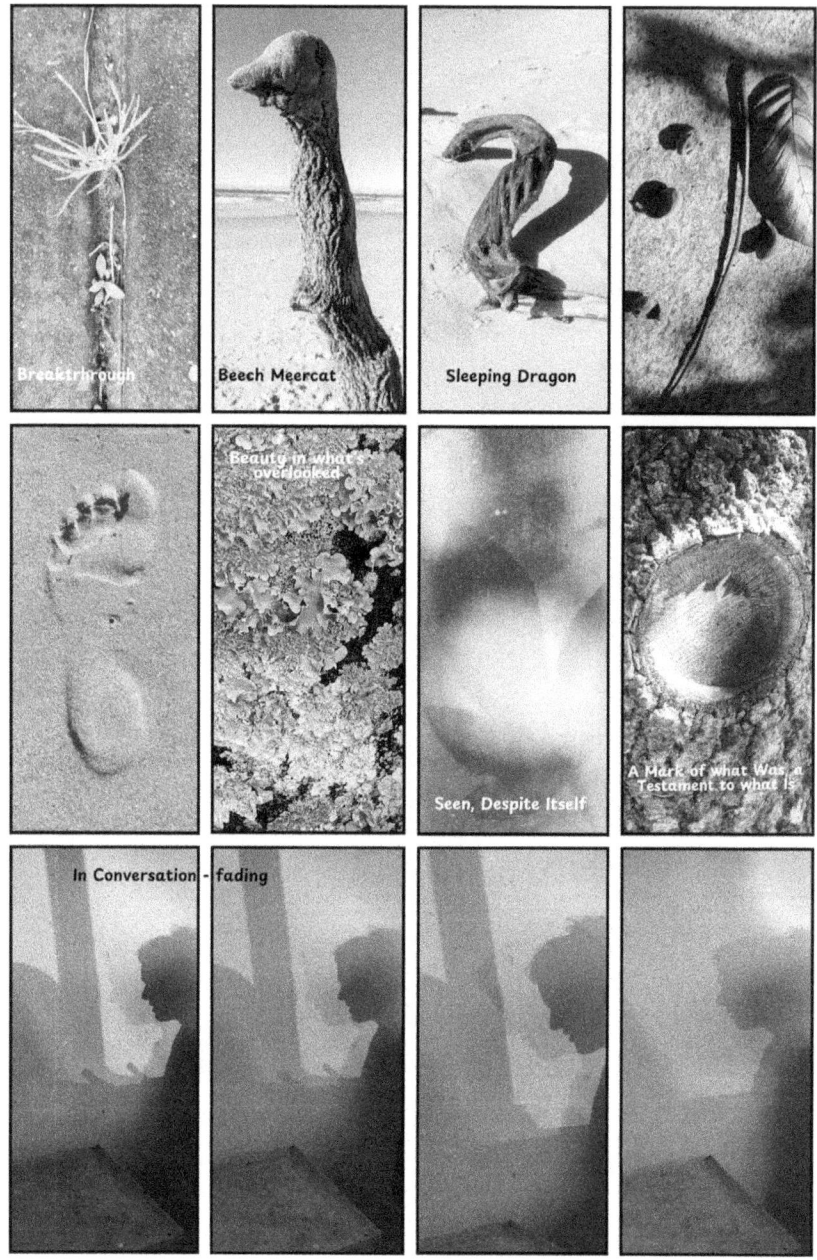

Image 13 **"Nature: The Ultimate Artist"** – Artworks by the author

Cultural Currents: Flowing Through Us

*"Creative expression draws from many waters —
influence, memory, longing, and lineage."*

– Flow-Inspired Reflection

Culture as a Creative Lens

Culture moves through us like a still river, guiding our steps in ways we don't always realise. It lingers in the warmth of a familiar greeting, in the scent of a beloved recipe drifting through the air. It's woven into the symbols we hold close, the rituals that anchor us in time, the unspoken rhythms that make us feel at home. Like a thread running through the fabric of our days, culture both grounds us and colours the way we see the world.

And yet, culture is not a single thread but a tapestry — woven from countless influences, both seen and unseen. Each of us carries a mosaic of cultural influences — some inherited from the broader society we live in, others deeply anchored in the personal culture of our families. These influences manifest in customs, stories, and traditions passed down through generations. When we reflect on these layers of culture, we open pathways for deeply personal and authentic creativity. Whether through art, food, or a treasured family tradition, our cultural heritage holds the potential to guide our Flow-Inspired Creations in meaningful ways.

Take a moment to reflect: What symbols, rituals, or practices have been passed down to you? How might these elements find their way into your creative process? Culture isn't just about history — it's a vibrant, living force that allows us to explore not only our individual stories but also the collective history that connects us all.

For me, the connection between culture and creativity was sparked during my time in Rajasthan, India. Imagine a bustling market alive with colour — golden turmeric, embroidered saris, the jingling of ankle bells. Amidst this sensory feast, I was captivated by the *Marwari* mural art adorning homes and temples. These vivid, centuries-old paintings seemed to pulse with life, telling stories of the land, the people, and their shared traditions. Equally enchanting was the music that filled the streets — musicians playing traditional melodies with a carefree, joyful abandon that seemed to echo the spirit of Rajasthan itself. The notes of their instruments pulsed with the same energy as the colours in the murals, weaving an auditory tapestry that added to the vibrancy of the moment.

Before India, I didn't feel a strong sense of cultural belonging. Growing up, I struggled to define what culture meant to me. While the Swiss language, customs, and landscapes had left their imprint, I often felt a sense of disconnection — like

I was searching for a thread to weave it all together. But Rajasthan offered a source of inspiration that bridged this gap. The vibrancy of its art, the symbolism embedded in its murals, and the way every stroke seemed to carry the weight of tradition helped me see the profound bond between culture and creativity.

I've come to understand that culture is never static. It moves and evolves with us, absorbing new places, ideas, and traditions along the way. This blending of influences can enrich our creativity. Engaging with culture creatively reveals the richness of our heritage, while opening us to the diversity of perspectives around us. Through culture, we honour where we come from, direct where we're going, and weave a tapestry of narratives that connect the personal with the collective, the past with the future.

Immersed in Culture: How India Steered My Course

Before we arrive in Rajasthan, let me take you back even further — to a memory from childhood, where my fascination with culture and difference first began to take shape.

From as far back as I can remember, I've been captivated by the unusual, drawn to things that were unique and strikingly different from what I knew. As a little girl, my favourite doll was dark-skinned, and she never left my side. She wasn't just a toy; she was a symbol of my curiosity and fascination with cultures beyond my own. I would drape myself in scarves, imagining exotic lands and bustling marketplaces, dreaming of lives steeped in customs and rituals I couldn't yet understand.

This curiosity grew stronger after I arrived in Australia. Adjusting to a new country and culture, learning English, and completing my missed education were all significant milestones that paved the way for my next chapter. After successfully graduating from TAFE (community college) with my High School Certificate at 26 years of age, as a mature age student, I enrolled in university to study philosophy. During a second-year elective in Eastern Philosophy, my world began to shift — slowly, but unmistakably.

These teachings, rich with ideas of interconnectedness and the unseen forces that unite us, opened my eyes to fresh perspectives on understanding myself and the world. They nurtured a trust not only in myself but also in the intricate web of life — a dynamic and ever-changing flow that I began to feel deeply connected to.

One year before completing my BA in philosophy, life shifted course, calling me back to Switzerland to be near my ailing mother. Initially, I lived in Zurich, and later moved to Geneva. All the while, the spark ignited by my studies in Eastern thought stayed with me, urging me to delve deeper. In 1979, driven by an unshakable longing to experience these philosophies firsthand, I travelled to India alone for the first time. What awaited me was unlike anything I could have imagined.

India was a collision of contrasts — visceral, vivid, and unforgettable. It was chaotic and overwhelming, yet profoundly beautiful. From that first trip, I was hooked. Each year, I returned — magnetised by its pull — to immerse myself in a kaleidoscope of cultures, traditions, and wisdom. In India, the stark contrasts of extreme poverty and immense wealth lived side by side, influencing my understanding in ways I hadn't expected.

But as I shared in *Verse and Flow*, not all moments were easy. My skin colour — a reminder of colonial history — sometimes placed me in the path of resentment and pain. Yet even then, India offered me an unexpected gift — the beginning of understanding that belonging is not always given freely by others, but can be consciously claimed from within.

Each year, after six months in India, I returned to Geneva to work with an American IT firm as an independent HR contractor — a position I held, remarkably, for almost 18 years. Equally unimaginable were the 18 years I spent alternating between these two worlds. Each return to India felt like stepping into a completely different rhythm. In Mumbai, the air thickened with the mingling scents of curry, incense, and sweat, while the streets pulsed with ceaseless energy — vendors calling, taxis jostling, and life unfolding vibrantly at every turn.

Jodhpur, where I mostly stayed, seemed frozen in a different era, its pace of life far removed from the rapid currents of Geneva. India in those days, especially in smaller cities, felt as though it were a few decades behind the rest of the world. Each return to Switzerland required days of adjustment, not only to the brisk speed of life but to the stark contrast in how time itself seemed to flow. It was as if I were living two parallel lives, each offering its own lessons and pace.

Drawn to Jodhpur, Rajasthan, I found a second home at an Ayurveda and Yoga centre founded by an Indian academic I had met in Geneva. The semi-desert landscape, with its ochre dust and deep blue skies, stripped life to its essentials. Haunting Ragas, vibrant saris, and Bollywood songs blaring from rickshaws stirred something deep within me.

Rajasthan was a place where I came to appreciate life's simplest aspects. The scarcity of water and the frequent power outages — these daily challenges shifted my perspective. They awakened me to how much I had taken for granted and taught me to see abundance in the smallest gestures. The people I came to know exemplified *Atithi Bhava*[23], the idea of treating unexpected guests with the utmost care and reverence. Even when they had little, they shared generously, and their spirit left an indelible mark on my heart.

Beyond its deep cultural richness, India gave me something even more profound: a lens through which to view my own story. My difficult childhood, once a source of pain, became part of a larger narrative — one that had formed me into someone resilient and resourceful, someone open to the world. I began to see that the struggles I had endured were not merely hardships; they were the soil from which growth and strength could take root. My mother's death in 1988 left more questions than memories. Her absence became a quiet thread — shaping how I came to understand loss and strength.

In Rajasthan's vibrant culture, I found inspiration for flowcrafting, and in India's rhythms, I discovered a way to reframe my past. It was here that I saw the beauty in the unfolding and the resilience that had carried me through to the place I had arrived.

From Ancient Hands to Mine: Learning the Art of *Marwari* [9] Murals

Come with me for a moment to Rajasthan — to a story that has stayed with me ever since.

Baiji[24], the grandmother and revered elder of the household, welcomed me into her world and into a tradition steeped in time: the art of painting wall murals. These centuries-old murals, alive with mythological stories and cultural heritage, were slowly disappearing as the modern generation replaced them with whitewashed walls. Despite the limits of our shared language — gestures and the few words of *Marwari* I had learnt — *Baiji* taught me this ancient art, passing on a skill that her ancestors had preserved for generations.

Guided by her, I painted with natural dyes — rich ochres and earthy pigments — applied with matchstick-sized sticks. Together, we brought stories to life on the walls, recreating a world of tradition and meaning. In time, I had the privilege of painting a mural in Baiji's own home, a deeply moving experience that felt like a bridge between the past and my present. Through this, I became part of an ancient lineage of storytellers — connected across time through the language of mural art.

In the unhurried rhythm of painting, time dissolved. Hours passed unnoticed as I immersed myself in the flow of creation, each application of pigment a step deeper into the narrative. It wasn't just an act of painting — it was a state of being, where past, present, and future seemed to coexist in the richness of the unfolding story. This was Flow-Inspired Creation at its most profound: a timeless, immersive process that connected me to a place, its people, and something larger than myself.

These murals became lifelines, much like other Flow-Inspired Creations have throughout my life. When words failed, creativity offered its own language — a way to uncover the unknown, rediscover forgotten parts of myself, or unearth something new. *Marwari* art reframed my life, giving voice to untold stories within.

Where painted patterns had once held the stories of women's hands, rhythm and voice would soon offer another kind of expression — equally rooted in culture, equally transformative. From colour and pattern to rhythm and voice, I found that flow could take many forms, each one revealing something essential.

Sacred Notes: A Cultural Tapestry of Chanting

In Rajasthan, my explorations into culture deepened through the soul-stirring rhythms of traditional Indian music, where I discovered another profound Flow-Inspired Creation: Bhajans and Kirtans[10]. My teacher, a revered Marwari musician, was as strict as he was skilled. Beneath his stern exterior lay an unspoken kindness — a care anchored in his meticulous teaching methods. Lessons demanded precision in pronunciation, intonation, and rhythm, leaving no room for shortcuts.

Seated cross-legged on the cool stone floor, I played the air-activated harmonium, its bellows breathing life into the music. My teacher relentlessly drilled scales — *SA, RE, GA,*

MA, PA, DHA, NI, SA[25] — until they became second nature. He corrected mistakes in chanting immediately, and his nod of approval when I succeeded spoke louder than words.

Bhajans and Kirtans, passed down through oral tradition, helped me engage with music on a deeper, more intuitive level. Each chant carried layers of history and devotion, enveloping me in a centuries-old cultural tapestry. I still cherish a handwritten book of lyrics from those lessons. Later, I taught myself to accompany the chants on guitar, blending East and West in a way that felt honest and personal.

Through this experience, I gained more than musical skill. Patience, discipline, and a deep respect for tradition became lasting gifts. Although my harmonium now sits silent and my lyric book rests undisturbed, the essence of those lessons lingers.

Decades later, the Sanskrit Shlokas (stanzas) I learnt from a Brahmin teacher resurface effortlessly in moments of reflection. The chants remain vivid and etched in my memory. They echo the composure, devotion, and joy that flow from harmonising with a lineage both ancient and alive — a creative thread that has the capacity to unite us all.

Wherever You're Coming From

If you're feeling unsure about your cultural roots, know that you're not alone. For many of us, family history, geographical distance, or even a lack of connection to specific traditions can make cultural heritage feel distant or intangible. But engaging with flowcrafting through culture isn't about having all the answers or knowing every ancestral detail. If you do have a strong cultural heritage, that's wonderful, but if you don't, you can start exploring what resonates with you right now — whether it's something familiar or an influence you're only beginning to discover.

Start with a broader cultural setting: a community gathering that inspires you, a symbolic object that draws your eye, or a colour and pattern that stirs something within you. Each of these discoveries can become a stepping stone, guiding us toward a deeper sense of connection with our cultural identity, opening new doors to self-expression.

For some, cultural identity doesn't fit neatly into one box. Maybe your experiences are influenced by several cultures, blending traditions, languages, or heritages in ways that make you feel uniquely you. In this richness lies creative potential. Let yourself celebrate this diversity. Mix and match colours, symbols, or practices from different influences to create something entirely your own. Flowcrafting invites us to honour all facets of our identity, crafting something deeply personal that moves freely beyond any single cultural tradition.

Even if cultural heritage doesn't immediately feel like a source of inspiration, take a moment to reflect on the subtle ways it might already influence you. What foods do you gravitate toward? What music moves you? What stories or traditions have been passed down, even if informally? Often, we carry cultural influences without fully realising it, woven into family rituals, community practices, or even our taste for certain fragrances, colours or patterns. These delicate threads can become a rich source of creativity, adding layers of meaning to your flowcrafting practice.

A Playful Song with a Lasting Lesson

Before we dive into practical exercises to explore cultural roots, I'd like to share a playful piece of my Swiss heritage that has stayed with me throughout the years. I only recently remembered this song as I was writing this chapter, and I want to share it with you.

This snippet from the Swiss-German song *"Dr Hans im Schnäggeloch"*[26] brings back cherished memories of my *Grossmueti* (grandmother). She would sing this whimsical tune whenever I found myself wanting something I couldn't have or turning down something I was offered. The playful lyrics carry a simple but profound lesson: the challenge of finding contentment and appreciating what we have, rather than longing for what we don't. (You'll find the words, translation and musical notation of this song in the End Notes of this book.)

Flowcrafting Your Cultural Story

I invite you now to explore your cultural heritage through the lens of Flow-Inspired Creations. What stories, symbols, or traditions feel most meaningful to you? How might they flow into your unique creative expressions — through art, music, writing, or another medium? As you engage with this practice, ask yourself: *What does my culture reveal about who I am?* What role have other cultural influences played in my life? Let your creations bring to light subtle links — inviting you to reimagine the narratives that affect how you move through the world, and guiding you into deeper understanding of your inner self and unique gifts.

Centring Exercise: Connecting and Aligning with Cultural Roots

As with previous exercises, before we begin to flow with culture, let's take a moment to ground ourselves. Centring helps open the door to flow, creativity, and reflection, allowing us to connect and align with our cultural heritage in a meaningful way.

1. **Find Your Space**: Sit comfortably in a quiet, undisturbed place. Close your eyes, relax your shoulders, and take a few deep breaths, grounding yourself in the present moment.

2. **Bring to Mind Your Heritage**: With each inhale, imagine connecting with your cultural heritage — symbols, traditions, fragrances, or even feelings that resonate with you. Let them fill your mind and heart, easing into whatever arises.

    If your cultural heritage doesn't come easily, allow yourself to feel, imagine or visualise images, fragrances, colours, shapes, or symbols you're naturally drawn to and invite them into your presence.

3. **Set Your Intention**: Silently affirm your desire to honour and explore your cultural origins in conversation with Flow-Inspired Creations. Approach this practice with curiosity, letting go of any assumptions or expectations.

4. **Open to Discovery**: As you complete this moment of centring, open your eyes and bring a sense of curiosity into the exercises.

Reflection and Creative Expressions

1. **Cultural Symbols: Finding Inspiration in Meaningful Icons**
   Identify a symbol, colour, or pattern from your own culture, your family heritage, or another culture that speaks to you. What does it represent? Sketch, write, or record your thoughts about this symbol and how it connects to your personal story. Let it inspire a flowcrafted piece — whether it's sound, visual, written, or even a collage or another expression of your choice.

2. **Rituals and Traditions: Stories Passed Down**
   Think about a cultural or family tradition that has influenced who you are. How does it inspire or ground you? Use this as a starting point for a flowcrafting activity. For example, create a visual representation of the tradition or express its essence through writing, music or movement. It could also be an edible inspiration, a culinary ritual, or a fragrance.

3. **Cultural Connections: Blending Influences**
   Reflect on how cultural experiences have influenced your habits, creativity, or worldview. Perhaps it's

the way you see time, the gestures you use, or the rhythms you live by. Translate these connections into a tactile, sound, visual or written narrative. Or you may discover your own way of translating this into flowcrafting. Consider how these elements guide your unique creative flow.

In the Current of Creative Expressions

Visual Storytelling: Symbols in Motion
Choose a symbol or pattern, either from your cultural heritage or a culture you feel drawn to. Create a story through drawing, painting, or arranging a collage. Or, if you prefer, you may want to write in your journal. Focus on the process, letting your hands move naturally. Notice how your creation evolves and how it connects you to who you are.

Soundscapes: Stories Told Through Music
Select a song, chant, or melody that ties you to your culture or a culture you feel drawn to. Close your eyes and immerse yourself in its sound and rhythm. Let the music inspire movement, drawing, or writing. Reflect on the emotions and stories it brings to life as it flows through you.

Embodied Stories: Movement as a Cultural Language
Explore a cultural gesture, dance, or traditional movement. Let your body interpret the story,

focusing on the experience rather than precision. Reflect on the connection between the movement and your cultural roots.

Uncovering Layers with Words
Begin with a memory, ritual, or story from your cultural background or another cultural background you're drawn to. Let your thoughts flow into written words, spoken reflections, or visual storytelling. Transform these reflections into another form — perhaps a poem, sketch, or spoken piece — or even by cooking up a storm! Let this process reveal new insights about your cultural narrative.

Sharing Your Experience
I'd love to hear what this exploration sparked for you. If you feel called to share, you're warmly invited to visit www.flow-inspired-creations.com.au to join the conversation.

Snapshot: A Heritage Remembered, A Story Rewoven

This blended story illustrates how flowcrafting from within a cultural lens can foster self-discovery and connection, guiding someone toward a cultural identity they never had the chance to fully know — until now. Let's call the main character Liam.

It wasn't until the age of 35 that Liam began to make sense of his unique way of being in the world — a realisation that offered unexpected relief and clarity. Raised in a foster home in urban Australia, he often felt out of sync with his peers, finding solace in creativity. While his birth culture was part of his lineage, it remained out of reach for most of his life — an unspoken absence marked by unanswered questions and missing threads.

A family reunion with members of his birth community changed that, unveiling the vibrant tapestry of symbols, stories, and a deep connection to nature that are part of his heritage. Inspired, Liam began exploring his identity through flowcrafting, blending storytelling with personal interpretation. Using a visual journal, he combined intuitive patterns, colours, and symbols drawn from his heritage and personal discoveries. Flowing water became a recurring motif, symbolising continuity and movement, while his unique lines and colours marked his path of discovery.

Flow-Inspired Creations brought Liam clarity and grounding. The process honoured his spontaneous, intuitive style, infusing his art with vibrancy — transforming it into a unique creative expression. Over time, this creative practice reframed how he viewed himself and his heritage, layering them into a narrative that truly felt like his own.

Liam's art became a bridge between his inner world and cultural background. Sharing his work brought connections with others, resonating deeply within his community. For Liam, cultural flowcrafting became a way to reclaim what had once been out of reach — not just his heritage, but a deeper sense of belonging, resilience, and self-understanding.

Closing Thought: Tracing Culture, Crafting Our Stories

This chapter reflects on culture as a connection to something greater than ourselves. It also explores culture as a lens for Flow-Inspired Creations and self-discovery — a vibrant source of inspiration that can guide our identities and sense of belonging. Through symbols, sounds, movements, food, and stories, culture invites us to bring to light our heritage and review or rewrite our narratives in meaningful ways.

Reflecting on my experiences in Rajasthani and *Marwari* culture, I shared how painting murals and learning traditional chanting deepened my understanding of cultural flowcrafting. These encounters revealed how creativity and heritage intertwine, illuminating our stories and guiding the way we engage with the world.

The exercises in this chapter encourage exploration of cultural heritage — its symbols, stories, and traditions — brought to life through flowcrafting. This practice is about immersing oneself in the process, trusting the flow, and letting it guide what emerges.

Flowcrafting in conversation with culture helps us attune to broader perspectives. It deepens connection, uncovers rich, invisible aspects of ourselves, and reveals ever more authentic ways to express the fullness of who we are.

Threads to Carry Forward

1. **Culture as Inspiration**: Recognising how our cultural heritage influences our creativity, offering unique layers of meaning to explore and celebrate.

2. **The Power of Reflection**: Connecting with the latent stories within our cultural roots — or another culture that inspires us — by drawing on Flow-Inspired Creations to explore the traditions and practices that speak to us.

3. **Presence in the Process**: Trusting in the open-ended practice of cultural flowcrafting, valuing presence and process over any fixed outcomes or expectations.

Let these reflections inspire you as you continue to craft your narrative, weaving together the threads of your heritage, your creativity, and your self-expression into a story that only you can tell.

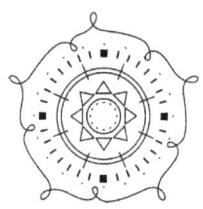

Cultural Currents: Flowing Through Us

Image 14 **"Cultural Currents"** – A flowcrafted collage by the author, blending digital fragments and visual elements to reflect the layered textures of identity, memory, and belonging.

Epilogue: Flowcrafting Tomorrow's Stories

This is where flow has brought me — not to a conclusion, but to a space of wonder. A place where imagination rises, where stories are no longer bound by who we've been, but shaped by who we dare to become. You're not alone on this path. You never were. Together, we keep weaving — not towards perfection, but towards possibility.

What I've learnt along the way is that creation is about choosing to respond to change with curiosity — to pause in the in-between, to let the unfamiliar speak, and to shape something new with our own hands and minds.

Flow is rarely loud. Often, it hums beneath the surface — in a single brushstroke, a sentence that surprises, or the way your body moves when no one's watching. Sometimes it arrives when all else has been tried — not with answers, but with a steady thread, a subtle direction, a way forward when the map remains unclear.

Belonging often begins quietly — in those moments when we stop asking if we are too much or not enough, and begin instead to ask: what is genuine and true? What have I always known, deep down, that's been waiting to take shape?

Every flowcrafting moment — every pattern drawn, word written, movement followed — is a kind of homecoming. Not to a place, but to yourself. A whisper of home that threads through your hands and settles in your being.

So no, this isn't an ending. It's an opening. A calm turning toward what's next.

You don't need permission to begin. You don't need to wait until it's perfect, or you're ready, or you feel whole. Your story is already in motion. Your hands already know the way.

Let them move. Let them make. Let them remember.

Flow will meet you there.

This is my offering, my way of stepping into flow. What will yours be?

Epilogue: Flowcrafting Tomorrow's Stories

Where Flow Finds Us

As we grow, so does creativity —
shifting, stretching, evolving,
adapting to meet us where we are.

Through uncertain terrain,
new doors opening, old ones closing,
we form, reform, and reimagine
the stories we tell ourselves.

Flow is both mirror and guide —
revealing strengths unspoken,
potentials yet to rise,
parts of us still waiting to be known.

When the path ahead is veiled,
flow becomes the steady ground,
the quiet hum of clarity,
the gentle glow that shows the way.

And when life steadies,
flow becomes a playground —
a place for wild ideas to run free,
for dreams to leap beyond the edges,
for limitless creation to unfold.

No matter where we stand
on the map of life,
flow is ours to step into,
to shape, to craft, to make our own —

Uniquely You

a story ever-unfolding,
a future waiting to be sung.

This is me, embracing my own flow — unapologetically, uniquely. And now, I invite you to do the same. Let yourself play. Let yourself be bold. However it wants to take shape, however imperfect it may seem — your expression is yours to claim.

*Beyond every ending is a space of wonder.
A place where imagination takes flight.*

> *There comes a time when readiness stirs,
> not loud, but clear.
> What once felt safe
> now lifts like wings at the edge of becoming.*
> *– Flow-Inspired Reflection*

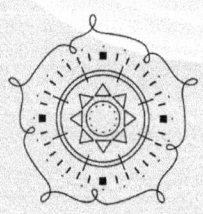

Epilogue: Flowcrafting Tomorrow's Stories

If something within you has stirred — a deeper trust, a quiet yes — let it unfold. Let it guide you toward a fuller expression of who you are and who you're becoming.

It's a bold path, this choosing to stand in your difference. To see it not as a reality to fix or mask, but as a sacred distinctiveness. A truth that holds a gift.

Perhaps you've discovered new ways to express yourself, or found a deeper connection to your inner world. Perhaps you've begun to see your story with fresh eyes — recognising the beauty in the parts that once felt uncertain or unseen.

Whatever has sparked within you, keep the dreaming going. Keep creating with flow. Keep thriving — just as you are.

Saying *yes* to the question on the front cover — *What if your difference is your greatest gift?* — is a brave act. It asks you to trust your uniqueness, to stand tall where you are, and to create not in spite of your difference, but because of it.

That's what flowcrafting invites. A deepening into what's already within you. A quiet expansion. A return to yourself.

And as you continue on your explorations, I offer you this final reflection — a flow-inspired parting gift.

Unwritten Skies — An Offering for Your Path Ahead

It begins in a breath — unnoticed, almost — until something inside you turns toward light. It doesn't announce itself. It rises like memory through the body. A flicker of ease in your chest. A thought, once afraid, daring to step forward.

Flow doesn't arrive like a map. It emerges like a thread — something half-remembered, fully felt. You don't follow it because you're certain; you follow because it stirs something true — in the lines you sketch without thinking, in the words you nearly didn't say. In the pull toward something unnamed but unmistakably yours.

This is the rhythm of becoming — not a finish line, but a wide, shimmering path unfolding under your feet as you walk it. There is no improved you waiting out there — only the natural unfolding of the real you, here.

Keep creating. Keep asking. Keep listening for the shape that wants to emerge through your hands.

This rhythm of becoming continues in the *Unwritten Skies* bonus offer — available for free at the end of this book.

The story isn't over.
In many ways, it's only just begun.

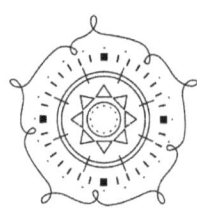

About the Author

Ruth Brunner (Grad Dip Couns, MCouns/Hons.) is an author, counsellor, creative guide, and mentor with over 25 years of experience in the fields of counselling and family therapy. Her work has taken place across diverse settings — from disability organisations and paediatric healthcare to trauma support and carer networks. In private practice, she has walked alongside individuals and families as they navigate life's challenges, reframe limiting narratives, and reconnect with their inner strengths.

At the heart of Ruth's work is a deep belief in the unique gifts each person carries — and the transformative power of creative flow. Her passion for self-expression and healing through creativity emerges from her own lived experience of feeling "outside the mould." Raised in a children's home in

Switzerland, Ruth grew up with early messages of not being "good enough" and often felt a deep sense of not belonging. Yet, rather than conforming, she followed an inner knowing — one that led her across continents, through new languages and cultures, and ultimately back to her own creative voice.

In 2020, Ruth stepped away from her counselling practice to pursue a creative Honours thesis at Southern Cross University. This autoethnographic exploration of creativity, identity, and self-expression laid the foundation for her first book, *Uniquely You*.

Through personal storytelling and flowcrafting — her chosen phrase for the intuitive, creative practices she calls Flow-Inspired Creations — Ruth invites readers to align with inner flow, embrace their difference, and reimagine the stories they tell themselves.

Now based in an Ecovillage in Western Australia, Ruth offers group and individual guidance to help others transform feelings of "not fitting in" into stories of empowerment and belonging. Her work encourages people to align with what's true, create with courage, reframe old narratives, and thrive — not by changing who they are, but by becoming more of who they've always been.

Learn more at: www.flow-inspired-creations.com.au

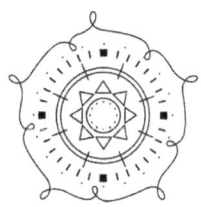

Acknowledgements

To all the Creative Navigators and Quiet Trailblazers — the dreamers, the doers, the questioners, and the creators.

This book exists because of you. Your courage to explore, reframe, and create lights the way for others, showing that every story — including yours — is worth celebrating. Thank you for embodying the resilience of bamboo in the wind — not a rigid strength, but the quiet power of bending, adapting, and flourishing through life's challenges.

I am deeply grateful to everyone who supported this pilgrimage — from the mentors who inspired me, to the friends and readers who believed in this work, to the community that continues to uplift and connect.

Special thanks to Dr Rob Garbutt, whose mentorship during my Honours Thesis — an autoethnographic exploration that laid the foundation for this book — was instrumental in shaping my understanding of narrative and creative self-expression. His thoughtful guidance and encouragement have left a lasting imprint on my evolution. I am also grateful to him for contributing his voice to this book through the *foreword*.

My heartfelt appreciation also goes to my first readers, Annie C., Rashmi P., Nadia R., and Shannon Anima, for taking the time to engage with my manuscript and offering thoughtful reflections that helped shape this book. Your insights, encouragement, and generosity of spirit have been invaluable. A special thanks to Rashmi for her patience and keen eye in reviewing the many book mock-up designs I created, and to Shannon for her beautiful *endorsement*.

I also want to acknowledge the behind-the-scenes supports that made this creative process more easeful — Canva for visual design, my human editors for their thoughtful insights, and AI tools that helped refine structure and grammar, especially when dyslexic hurdles asked me to move more slowly. These supports didn't replace my voice — they helped me clarify and express it more clearly. What's on the page remains deeply personal and entirely my own.

Finally, to you, the reader — thank you for joining me on this journey through *Uniquely You*. Writing this book has been a deeply personal experience, and knowing it may resonate with or support you fills me with a profound sense of fulfilment. Your willingness to explore Flow-Inspired Creations and embrace your uniqueness is a testament to your courage and creativity.

May this book be a companion on your path, offering encouragement, fresh perspectives, and a celebration of all that makes you uniquely you.

From Story to Offering

This book was the beginning of something — not just for me, but I hope, for you too.

Through the writing of *Uniquely You*, new conversations have begun — around creativity, identity, voice, and belonging. These conversations are now taking shape as live gatherings, reflective spaces, and ongoing ways to explore what's unfolding.

How This Work Continues

While this book closes, the conversation it began continues — now through shared spaces, spoken reflections, and creative presence.

On the following pages, you'll find a few of the speaking topics I now share — along with other pathways for engaging with this work — all shaped by the threads explored within these pages.

Flowing Into Conversation
with Ruth Brunner

A counsellor, creative guide, and author of *Uniquely You*, Ruth supports those who've long felt out of step with the world, to reclaim voice, rhythm, and belonging. With over 25 years of counselling and coaching experience, and a lived story of not quite fitting the mould, she offers a new narrative: one where difference becomes a quiet strength.

Her talks invite reflection, creative reconnection, and the unfolding of self-expression — drawn from her work with Flow-Inspired Creations.

Speaking Topics:

1. The Foundational Message — From Self-Protection to Self-Expression
Theme: Releasing the pressure to adapt in order to fit in, and returning to your natural rhythm.
Core Message: There's power in choosing not to fit in — and reclaiming a path shaped by your own way of being and truth.

2. The Creativity Thread — Create as You Are
Theme: How intuitive, pressure-free creative practices can become a gateway to self-acceptance and self-expression.
Core Message: When creativity is freed from outcomes, it can mirror the self that's been waiting beneath the pressure to conform.

3. The Belonging Thread — Where Belonging Begins Within
Theme: Redefining belonging as something that begins with how we relate to ourselves, not how well we fit into external norms.
Core Message: True belonging doesn't require us to be less sensitive, less expressive, or more polished — it asks us to come home to ourselves.

For Speaking Enquiries or Creative Collaborations:
hello@flow-inspired-creations.com.au

What Waits Beyond These Pages

Sometimes a book ends, but something in you is just beginning. If you're curious to keep exploring — to deepen, express, or simply be met — there's space for that.

Below are **three pathways** you're welcome to follow — in your own way, in your own time

🕸 Free Companion Guide: *Unwritten Skies*

A gift to help you reflect on what's shifted — and reimagine what's next, created to meet you wherever you are — with prompts to align, create, reframe, and thrive.

Starting with the insight:

* Our thoughts shape our worlds — and the worlds we shape can free us.

If *Uniquely You* stirred something within you — a softened story, a clearer voice, or the yet unspoken beginnings of change — this guide offers a way to deepen that shift.

Unwritten Skies invites you to pause, reflect, and expand — and continue deepening the inner growth that's already begun.

✦ What's Inside
- ∞ A prompt to revisit what's shifted
- ∞ A reflection to view your story from a broader perspective
- ∞ A space to consider what you're becoming — without any pressure
- ∞ A silent affirmation: you are already in motion

✦ This guide is part of the evolving **B.E.C.O.M.E. Experience** — alongside the bonus gift *A Room of Your Own Making* offered at the beginning of this book.

Download your **free copy here**:
- ☐ https://www.flow-inspired-creations.com.au/unwritten-skies/

These QR codes can take a moment to load — thanks for your patience.

🕸 Continue the Journey: The B.E.C.O.M.E. Experience

A creative path to inner belonging, self-expression, and becoming.

If you feel called to go deeper — into creativity, authenticity, and a growing sense of belonging — The B.E.C.O.M.E. Experience offers a six-week process anchored in flow, reflection, and self-expression.

This creative exploration supports your unique becoming — not by changing who you are, but by aligning with the truth of who you've always been.

Each stage invites you to meet well-worn stories with curiosity and compassion, embrace your voice, and begin to embody the freedom to live as you are.

If you feel drawn to explore this six-week experience, you can visit the link below to find out more and express your interest.

✦ **Learn more or express interest here:**
- ☐ https://www.flow-inspired-creations.com.au/become-offer-journey/

🕸 Personalised Support & Mentorship

For those drawn to one-on-one mentorship and reflection, Ruth offers personalised coaching — a calm space to pause, reconnect, and move at your own pace through the terrain explored in *Uniquely You* and your own personal unfolding.

These sessions offer a blend of guidance, deep listening, and companioning — meeting you where you are and honouring what's ready to emerge.

✦ **Learn more or express interest here:**
- https://www.flow-inspired-creations.com.au/mentoring-11-support/

When QR codes take their time to load — have a cuppa (or take a deep breath).

✦ Ways to Stay in Touch

I'll be sharing updates, reflections, and offerings on the blog — a space for news, creative sparks, and staying in touch. You're welcome to visit anytime, and if something resonates, you're invited to leave a comment or share your own reflections.

https://www.flow-inspired-creations.com.au/#blog

Follow along (if it feels right):

- ☐ **Website**: www.flow-inspired-creations.com.au (QR code also available on the back cover)

- ☐ **LinkedIn**: www.linkedin.com/in/ruth-brunner-author

- ☐ **Instagram | Facebook | Pinterest**: @flowinspiredcreations

The book may be drawing to a close, but your becoming continues.

Uniquely You

However you move forward, may it be with ease, curiosity, and the calm confidence that your difference was always something to be honoured.

From one Creative Navigator to another,
Ruth
Flow-Inspired Creations –
Where Belonging Begins Within

End Notes

End notes are referenced close to terms in the text to support ease of reading and quick access to meaning.

[1] Inner Flow

The concept of inner flow, introduced by psychologist Mihály Csíkszentmihályi, describes a state of complete absorption in an activity, where focus is effortless, time seems to disappear, and actions feel naturally aligned. This optimal state enhances creativity, performance, and overall well-being, making challenges feel engaging rather than overwhelming.

Connecting with one's inner flow can bring:

- Greater clarity — helping us navigate challenges with a sense of ease.
- Increased creativity — allowing ideas to emerge naturally.
- A sense of fulfillment — as the process itself becomes intrinsically rewarding.
- Alignment with self — where our unique rhythm and way of being feel in sync with what we create.

[2] **Dan Sullivan** co-founder of Strategic Coach, introduced the concept of *"The Gap and The Gain."* This framework encourages focusing on personal growth and progress (the gain) rather than

on unmet goals or perceived shortcomings (the gap), fostering gratitude, resilience, and a more positive mindset.

[3] **Alphorn:** A traditional Swiss musical instrument, typically made of wood and several meters long, used historically by herdsmen in the Alps to communicate across great distances and now often played in Swiss cultural and musical events. My Grossvati (Grandfather) used to play the Alphorn, and its sound remains a cherished memory from my childhood.

[4] ***Wartheim***, located in Muri bei Bern, was one of the first homes for "difficult to manage" children in Switzerland, founded in 1862. Over the years, its purpose evolved, originally serving as a facility for the "destitute", the ill, and those in need of correction or disciplinary care, before transitioning to a home focused on structured upbringing. In my time it was exclusively for girls, 25 of us. There were many transitions between then and now. Website of today's Wartheim — to learn more visit: www.wartheim.ch

[5] The Hidden History of *Verdingkinder*

While researching my family history for my Honours thesis, I uncovered a deeply unsettling chapter of Switzerland's past: the practice of *Verdingkinder*. These "contract children" were placed under guardianship by Swiss authorities, often taken from single parents or impoverished families, and forced into labour under harsh conditions. This systemic practice, rooted in the Swiss guardianship laws of the 20th century, remained a hidden scar in Switzerland's idyllic image until recent decades. Many of these individuals, some still alive today, have come forward to share their stories, revealing the hardships they endured.

In response, Swiss authorities offered a compensation fund, though many declined to claim it, either because they felt it wasn't enough or because revisiting the past was too painful. Learning about this history during my research was profoundly disturbing, especially as I realised I, too, had been part of this guardianship system, albeit in a different way. My experience in the children's home didn't involve forced labour, but the discovery of this broader context was a stark reminder of the societal judgment placed on children like me. If you want to read more, go to: https://www.bj.admin.ch/bj/en/home/gesellschaft/fszm.html

Despite the weight of these revelations, they only deepened my resolve to rise above societal judgment and to advocate for others who feel unseen or disenfranchised. This book is, in part, my way of turning those scars into a story of resilience, one that I hope inspires others to reimagine their own narratives.

[6] **Donna Haraway** is a scholar and feminist theorist known for her work on science, technology, and culture. Her influential essay, *A Cyborg Manifesto* (1985), challenges traditional boundaries between humans, machines, and animals, promoting new ways of thinking about identity, feminism, and interconnectedness.

[7] **Kintsugi:** A traditional Japanese art form that involves repairing broken pottery by mending the cracks with gold, silver, or lacquer mixed with powdered gold. Rather than hiding the flaws, Kintsugi celebrates them, turning the breakage into part of the object's history and beauty. It symbolizes resilience, transformation, and the idea that imperfections can add value and meaning.

[8] **Positive Constructive Daydreaming and Creativity**
Research into positive constructive daydreaming — a form of mind-wandering characterized by playful and imaginative thinking — suggests it can enhance creativity and problem-solving. This mental state engages the brain's default mode network (DMN), which is active during introspection and creative exploration. By allowing the mind to freely associate ideas in a relaxed state, positive constructive daydreaming fosters novel insights and artistic expression. For more on this phenomenon, see: Positive Constructive Daydreaming and Creativity. For more information, see: (https://www.frontiersin.org/journals/psychology/articles/10.3389/fpsyg.2013.00626/full)

[9] **Marwari**: A term referring to the people of the Marwar region in Rajasthan, India, known for their rich cultural heritage, entrepreneurial spirit, and distinct dialect of the Rajasthani language.

[10] **Bhajans and Kirtans**: Devotional songs in Indian spiritual traditions, often sung in praise of deities. Bhajans are reflective and melodic, while Kirtans are call-and-response chants, fostering collective spiritual connection.

[11] A fictionalised name to preserve privacy.

[12] **Dr. Dan Siegel**: A clinical professor of psychiatry at UCLA and a pioneer in interpersonal neurobiology. His works, such as *The Developing Mind* and *Mindsight*, highlight the brain's capacity for neuroplasticity, emphasizing how mindfulness and relationships can reshape the brain to support mental health and resilience.

[13] **Sheila Hicks**: An American artist and textile designer renowned for her innovative weaving and fibre art. Blending traditional craft with modern art, her works explore texture, colour, and form, often bridging the boundaries between fine art and design.

[14] **Zentangle®:** A trademarked method of drawing structured patterns developed by Maria Thomas and Rick Roberts. Zentangle is known for promoting relaxation, focus, and creativity. While I've drawn inspiration from this method, I've adapted it to my own needs and approach — referring to it as *Flow-Inspired Creations* and *flowcrafting* with patterns.

[15] **Stephanie Dowrick**: A New Zealand-born writer, psychotherapist, and interfaith minister known for her books on spirituality, creativity, and personal transformation. Her works, such as *Creative Journal Writing* and *Choosing Happiness*, emphasize self-discovery, mindfulness, and the power of inner reflection.

[16] **Grossvati** is a Swiss German term that translates to "grandfather" in English. It is a warm and affectionate way to refer to one's grandfather in the Swiss German dialect, commonly used in Switzerland, particularly in the German-speaking regions.

[17] Fictionalised name to preserve privacy

[18] The **Bärengraben** (Bear Pit) in Bern, Switzerland, is a historic enclosure where bears — symbols of the city — were kept for centuries. Originally located in the centre of town, near the Nydegg Bridge, it served as a tourist attraction and a nod to Bern's emblematic animal. In recent years, the bears were relocated to a more spacious and natural habitat on the outskirts of the city, known as the BearPark (*BärenPark*), providing them with a better quality of life while maintaining their cultural significance.

[19] **Ali Haigh** is a contemporary Australian printmaker and designer based in New South Wales. She draws inspiration from the natural patterns and shapes found in her coastal surroundings, translating these observations into playful and joyful designs. Ali's creative journey includes the "Collaborate365" project, where she created an ephemeral artwork daily for a year, fostering a deep connection with nature and her community. Beyond her artistic practice, Ali contributes to community projects, including her role as Arts Coordinator. Learn more at: www.alihaigh.com

[20] **Olafur Eliasson** is a renowned Danish-Icelandic artist celebrated for his immersive installations and sculptures that explore light, perception, and the natural world. His works often combine art, science, and environmental awareness, inviting audiences to experience and reflect on their surroundings. Notable projects include *The Weather Project* (2003) at Tate Modern and *Your Rainbow Panorama* (2011) in Denmark. Learn more about his work at: www.olafureliasson.net.

[21] **Wabi-Sabi** is a Japanese aesthetic and philosophical concept that embraces the beauty of imperfection, impermanence, and the natural cycle of growth and decay. Rooted in Zen Buddhism and traditional Japanese tea ceremonies, Wabi-Sabi values simplicity, asymmetry, and the quiet elegance of things that are weathered, aged, or incomplete. It invites us to appreciate life's fleeting nature and find meaning in the imperfect, making it a powerful perspective for creative expression and self-acceptance.

[22] **Andy Goldsworthy** is a British sculptor, photographer, and environmental artist known for creating site-specific works that integrate natural materials like stones, leaves, ice, and branches. His ephemeral and permanent installations highlight the beauty and impermanence of nature, often blending art with the surrounding environment. Goldsworthy's work invites viewers to reflect on the relationship between humanity and the natural world. To learn more, see: https://andygoldsworthystudio.com.

[23] **Atithi Bhava** is a Sanskrit term that translates to "guest attitude" or "the spirit of hospitality." Rooted in Indian culture, it emphasizes the importance of welcoming and honoring guests with warmth, generosity, and respect. This practice extends beyond mere etiquette, reflecting a deep value placed on human connection and mutual respect, often expressed in the phrase *"Atithi Devo Bhava"* — "The guest is like God."

[24] **Baiji**: In Rajasthan, India, the term *Baiji* is a respectful way to address a woman, often used to mean "sister" or "grandmother," depending on the context and relationship. It conveys both familial warmth and cultural reverence.

[25] **Indian Musical Scale (Sargam)** — The Indian musical scale, known as **Sargam**, consists of seven main notes: **SA, RE, GA, MA, PA, DHA, NI, SA**. These correspond to the Western solfège (**Do, Re, Mi, Fa, Sol, La, Ti, Do**) and form the foundation of Indian classical music. Used in both Hindustani (North Indian) and Carnatic (South Indian) traditions, these notes are essential in

End Notes

Bhajans and Kirtans, devotional singing practices that emphasize melody, rhythm, and spiritual connection.

[26] **Hans im Schnäggeloch** — the translation is: Hans in a place called Schnäggeloch has everything he wants! And what he has, he doesn't want. And what he wants, he doesn't have. Hans in Schnäggeloch has everything he wants!

German (Swiss-German/Alemannic)
Original lyrics

English
Translation

D'r Hans im Schnokeloch

Hans in Schnockeloch

D'r Hans im Schnòckeloch hät àlles, wàs er will!	Hans in Schnockeloch [1] has everything he wants!
Un wàs er hät, dess will er nit,	And what he has, he doesn't want.
Un wàs er will, dess hät er nit.	And what he wants, he doesn't have.
D'r Hans im Schnòckeloch hät àlles, wàs er will!	Hans in Schnockeloch has everything he wants!

D'r Hans im Schnokeloch

Notes

Uniquely You

Notes

www.ingramcontent.com/pod-product-compliance
Lightning Source LLC
Chambersburg PA
CBHW061229070526
44584CB00030B/4047